MY SENSORY BOOK

MY SENSORY BOOK:

Working Together to Explore Sensory Issues and the Big Feelings They Can Cause: A Workbook for Parents, Professionals, and Children

Lauren H. Kerstein, LCSW

Autism Asperger Publishing Co.
P.O. Box 23173
Shawnee Mission, Kansas 66283-0173
www.asperger.net

P.O. Box 23173
Shawnee Mission, Kansas 66283-0173
www.asperger.net • 913.897.1004

Publisher's Cataloging-in-Publication

Kerstein, Lauren H.
        My sensory book : working together to explore sensory issues and
        the big feelings they can cause : a workbook for parents,
        professionals, and children / Lauren H. Kerstein. -- 1st ed. --
        Shawnee Mission, Kan. : Autism Asperger Pub. Co., c2008.

                p. ; cm.
                ISBN: 978-1-934575-21-5
                LCCN: 2008924315

                Summary: An interactive workbook designed to help children
        with sensory issues learn how to identify their needs and develop
        strategies to address them. Also works on children's self-esteem.
                Includes bibliographical references.
                1. Senses and sensation in children. 2. Sensory integration
        dysfunction in children. 3. Sensory disorders in children. 4. [Senses
        and sensation.] I. Title.

RJ496.S44 K47 2008   2008924315
618.92/8588--dc22   0804

This book is designed in Frutiger and American Typewriter.

Printed in the United States of America.

DEDICATED TO

My dad – for being my biggest fan and teaching me so much. You always told me I could do something with my love of writing. I finally did it! You are sorely missed.

My mom – you give me the strength and love I need to pursue my dreams. Thank you for standing behind me every step of the way.

ACKNOWLEDGMENTS

This book wouldn't have been possible without the support of the following people. I want to first thank my editor, Kirsten McBride, for your insight, wisdom, thought-provoking feedback, and patience. You encouraged me to stretch beyond what I thought possible. Additional thanks to all of the wonderful staff at AAPC, including Vivian and Charla, for all of your hard work. To Tracy Murnan Stackhouse, thank you for sharing your knowledge and time.

Thank you to Aunt Ellen for showing me that writing a book and getting it published is possible. I want to extend my gratitude to Suzi, Stanley, Mimi, Ryan, Jenna, Uncle Jon, Ester, Cheryl, Megan, Rob, David, and Wendy for all of your support.

Thank you to my sister Amy for helping me to clarify my thoughts and offering support and assistance.

To all of the children, adolescents, and families with whom I have had the privilege of spending time: You are amazing and have enriched my life so much. Thank you.

I want to extend a special thank you to my husband, Josh, for your support and encouragement as I follow my writing dreams. I couldn't do it without you.

Finally, I want to thank my daughters, Sarah and Danielle, for sharing your mommy with the computer. You both have spent your fair share of time on my lap as I typed away. I love you.

– L. H. K.

TABLE OF CONTENTS

WELCOME

Children working independently will be called Explorers from here on out. Adults assisting children (teachers, parents, occupational therapists, social workers, etc.) will be called Facilitators.

 Facilitator　　 **Explorer**

 A Note to Explorers: Hi, I am so excited you have picked up this book and begun to look through it. I hope the following map will help you get started and even enjoy it (yes, exploring your sensory body can be fun!). You might ask, "But isn't the Table of Contents a map?" The answer is yes, but I thought you might like a map that is a little easier to understand. So, here it is.

My Sensory Book Map

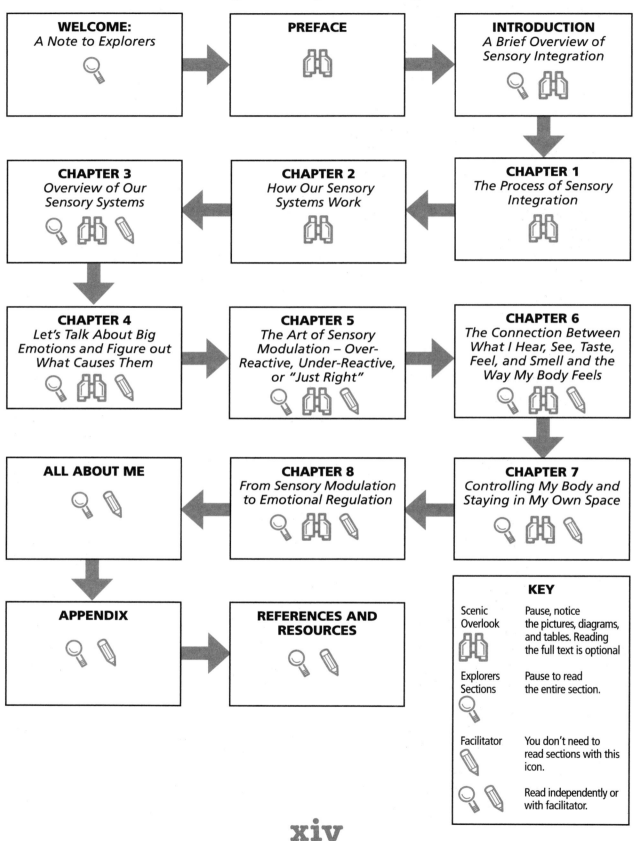

WELCOME:
A Note to Explorers

PREFACE

INTRODUCTION
A Brief Overview of Sensory Integration

CHAPTER 3
Overview of Our Sensory Systems

CHAPTER 2
How Our Sensory Systems Work

CHAPTER 1
The Process of Sensory Integration

CHAPTER 4
Let's Talk About Big Emotions and Figure out What Causes Them

CHAPTER 5
The Art of Sensory Modulation – Over-Reactive, Under-Reactive, or "Just Right"

CHAPTER 6
The Connection Between What I Hear, See, Taste, Feel, and Smell and the Way My Body Feels

ALL ABOUT ME

CHAPTER 8
From Sensory Modulation to Emotional Regulation

CHAPTER 7
Controlling My Body and Staying in My Own Space

APPENDIX

REFERENCES AND RESOURCES

KEY

Scenic Overlook — Pause, notice the pictures, diagrams, and tables. Reading the full text is optional

Explorers Sections — Pause to read the entire section.

Facilitator — You don't need to read sections with this icon.

Read independently or with facilitator.

PREFACE

The topic of sensory issues is popping up more and more in discussions about children's behavior and learning. With only a scant (albeit slowly growing) research base in this area, professionals argue over whether or not sensory integration issues are "real" and, therefore, whether we should attempt to address them and how. Whether you fall into the category of parents, teachers, or clinicians who have seen remarkable changes and improvements in children following work with an occupational therapist to address their sensory needs, or whether you fall into the category of people who dispute the benefits of recognizing sensory issues is irrelevant here. The reality is that there are increasingly large numbers of children struggling with "behavioral issues" who are not responding consistently to traditional methods of intervention.

This book was written to encourage clinicians, parents, teachers, and other professionals to step outside the box and look at the child as a whole person rather than only focus on his or her emotional and behavioral issues. We will explore sensory issues, sensory modulation, emotional modulation, and the relationship between the sensory and emotional systems.

About This Book

This workbook is designed as a tool to assist children in understanding their sensory systems better. It can be used with children ages 7 and up,[1] but given its visual nature, parts of it may be also be effective with younger children. It can be used in

---

[1] All ages listed throughout this workbook are meant as a guide only. Each child develops at his/her unique rate and may be able to do things earlier than suggested or may benefit from doing things later.

a general way or in specific situations. That is, you may choose to use it "in the moment," in preparation for an event, or in retrospect to review previous episodes.

The following is an example of using the book **in the moment**. Imagine that you have noticed that your child seems to consistently have trouble in restaurants but you have not yet determined why. Perhaps you are operating under the assumption that there is a sensory component to your child's challenges (or your child has been assessed as having sensory difficulties).

The next time you walk into a restaurant with your child, you can take a moment to focus on the different sensory stimuli that surround you. You may notice that the lights are dim, the smells are strong, and the noise from a birthday celebration in an adjoining room is loud. It may be very helpful to take a moment and talk through the different items your child notices in the restaurant (in addition to what you are noticing) and process the impact these stimuli may have on your child. You can do this at your table if you think the child can focus, or you can step outside for a moment to talk. During this conversation, you may link the different stimuli to particular feelings they may be causing. For example, the loud noises may elicit a feeling of nervousness as it is hard to predict when the noise will increase and when it will subside again. You can then come up with a plan that may help the child if his nervousness increases, as discussed later in this book.

You can also use the workbook **in preparation for an event** that may present stressful stimuli. For example, if the child is invited to a birthday party and you know the sounds will echo given the nature of the room where the party will take place, you can discuss strategies that may help mitigate the sounds or that might address the emotional reaction the child may have in response to the echoing, such as fear.

Finally, you can use the workbook **after the fact** to process an event that was particularly stressful for the child. For example, let's say your 5-year-old daughter had a dance recital earlier in the day and had been in a "bad mood" prior to the recital, hitting and throwing fits. As you think back, you remember that about halfway through the recital, the teacher asked the kids to do a costume change, and your child refused. It occurs to you that in addition to being nervous about performing, the anticipation of the texture of the costume may have been causing your child stress prior to the recital. You can use the workbook to process the stress and possible anxiety your daughter felt, look at the ways she chose to handle it, and discuss methods that may have more effectively solved the problem. You can also talk about the positive aspects of the event, such as the fact that your daughter was able to stay calm throughout the performance. When working with older children, it may be useful to ask them what they think helped them stay calm as this may generate strategy ideas for the future.

It is my hope that using this workbook will help children – and the adults who interact with them – to better understand sensory triggers, the impact these sensory triggers have on their bodies, feelings, and moods, and subsequently develop strategies that can regulate their emotional and physical reaction so they feel better and function better.

This workbook will help children and the adults with whom they interact to:

- Develop a better understanding of their sensory systems.

- Gain a better understanding of sensory and emotional triggers.

- Increase their awareness of which sensory triggers cause their bodies to over-react, under-react, or respond "just right."

- Determine if and when sensory triggers impact their feelings in negative and positive ways.

- Implement different interventions to determine which strategies are effective for different sensory triggers.

- Expand their understanding of what feelings they are experiencing, the intensity of those feelings, and what they can do to regulate their feelings to be in sync with a given situation.

It is my belief that we can help children feel more comfortable in their environments and the situations that arise if we can build an awareness of their emotional and sensory selves.

L. H. K.

INTRODUCTION

A BRIEF OVERVIEW OF SENSORY INTEGRATION

It was Saturday morning at around 11:00 o'clock, and Mira stood in the doorway of Joanne's Diner on her second day of work. She had been so excited to get a job as a waitress for the summer. It was her first summer job, and she really wanted to show her parents that she could make money and do things on her own. But now she stood paralyzed. She couldn't force herself to walk in any further. The smell of grease from the kitchen was so strong she thought she might throw up. On top of the horrible smell, the light over the pinball machine was flickering, the juke boxes seemed to all be playing simultaneously yet not in sync, and the child's birthday party in the center of the room was deafening.

Mira stepped back out of the diner to try to collect herself. She stood there, blood coursing through her veins, head pounding, and rather nauseous trying to figure *out what to do so she wouldn't lose her job. She just couldn't understand what her problem was but she also couldn't bring herself to walk back through the door.*

The literature about sensory integration is growing at a rapid pace, not only about sensory integration in general, but also about its role in a variety of developmental and learning issues, including those exhibited by many children with autism spectrum disorders. These issues include, but are not limited to, difficulty processing information accurately and smoothly, an inability to concentrate and focus, social challenges, lack of understanding of all aspects of emotions, and behavioral outbursts. Much research has also been conducted and continues to be conducted to more systematically identify the benefits of addressing issues in the sensory realm. (For a brief history of sensory integration, please see pages 149-150 in the Appendix.)

As a clinician working in schools, homes, and in my office, I have often questioned the use of the word *behavior*. As I learned more about sensory integration and more about emotional regulation, I began to design interventions that took both of these areas into account when trying to address behavioral issues. Prior to this shift, it seemed that many of the children with whom I worked continued to struggle (or struggled even more) after being exposed to traditional mental health techniques. While I don't in any way doubt the merit of any of the techniques I have used, and continue to use, in the mental health realm (including, but not limited to, cognitive behavior therapy, functional behavioral analysis, play therapy, systems work), I recognize the value of looking further at underlying causes of so-called "behavior" and infusing non-traditional mental health methods into my treatment. It is this combination of mental health approaches combined with other strategies, such as those in the sensory realm, that have paved the way for this book.

Note. Given my professional training, the information about sensory integration and its related components throughout this book is written by a mental health clinician, not an occupational therapist. This distinction is important as I am looking at sensory information through a mental health lens, shaped by experience working with children with behavioral challenges, developmental delays, social/emotional difficulties, and mental health issues. Although I have been trained by occupational therapists and have worked consistently on multi-disciplinary teams for nearly 12 years, my initial training was in the area of mental health.

It is my hope that with this workbook you will gain insights that will enable you to choose and design interventions that assist your child as a whole person rather than just as a child with behavioral difficulties. Further, these insights will undoubtedly inspire a paradigm shift that will strengthen the relationship between you and the child, increase the child's understanding of himself, and make life events more manageable.

A Note About Pronouns: I will be alternating using "he" and "she" throughout the book.

Sensory Processing and Sensory Integration

The deeper I dove into this book, the more I felt I was getting "caught" in the terminology. I began to wonder why some refer to sensory issues as "sensory processing disorder" while others use the term "sensory integration disorder or dysfunction."

I am making the assumption that you might struggle with this terminology as well, so I have included a brief description of the reason why some use the term "sensory processing" while others use "sensory integration." I am also including other terms you will encounter throughout this work, along with brief definitions and examples to illustrate what they "look like" in real life. All of these concepts and terms will be further expanded throughout the book.

Sensory integration is the overarching theory posed by Dr. Ayres in the 1970s to describe our ability to take information in from the environment and process, organize, and synthesize this input so as to formulate an adaptive response (Ayres, 1979) or effective plan of action. For example, if a 9-month-old baby hears an airplane but does not know what she is hearing, she might point to the airplane and look at her mom as if to say, "what is that?" In this scenario, the baby hears the sound of the airplane, the sound registers in her brain, and her brain sends back a message saying, "point to mommy and look at her." If a child has trouble integrating information in this manner, instead, he might cry, scream, look around but not actually locate the sound, or act out any combination of these maladaptive responses. As Dr. Ayres posited, **sensory issues can impact behavior, learning, and overall development.**

Following Ayres' seminal work related to sensory integration in 1979, a number of clinicians expanded upon her ideas. These expansions include, but are not limited to, (a) the development of screening measures and tools (Dunn, 2002; Dunn with Brown, 2002; Dunn 2006; Miller, 1982); (b) the design of various treatments (Wilbarger & Wilbarger, 1991; Williams & Shellenberger, 1996); and (c) the refinement of hands-on strategies and games for children struggling with sensory integrative issues in general (Kranowitz, 1998; Miller, 2006; Myles, Cook, Miller, Rinner, & Robbins, 2000; Williams & Shellenberger, 1996).

Following these advances in the field of sensory integration, Dr. Lucy Miller spearheaded an effort to expand the diagnostic vocabulary. In an article entitled *Position Statement on Terminology Related to Sensory Integration Dysfunction* (2004), Miller, Cermak, Lane, Anzalone, and Koomar attempted to clarify sensory terminology, adopting the term "sensory processing disorder" (SPD). Sensory processing disorder is used as an umbrella term that describes all forms of disorders within the sensory realm, including sensory modulation disorder, sensory discrimination disorder, and sensory-based motor disorder. Sensory modulation disorder is further divided into over-responsivity, under-responsivity, and sensory seeking. Sensory-based motor disorder includes dyspraxia (difficulty organizing one's body in order to execute a movement or series of motions) and postural disorders.

Miller also led a successful movement to include this diagnostic terminology in both the *Diagnostic Classification: Zero to Three: Diagnostic Classification of Mental Health in Developmental Disorders in Infancy and Early Childhood* (ICDL, 2006) and *Diagnostic Manual for Infancy and Early Childhood* (ICDL, 2007). Much rigorous research continues to be conducted to support the efficacy of interventions in the sensory realm in hopes that the diagnosis will be included in the DSM-V in 2012. (For more comprehensive information regarding SPD, please see http://www. spdfoundation.net/.)

Miller et al.'s (2004) attempts to clarify the disorder were received with mixed reviews in the field of occupational therapy. While some thought their efforts contributed to the field, others chose to continue to use Ayres' original term "sensory integration." It is outside the scope of this book to determine which of the two are more "accurate." For the purposes of this book, I will use "sensory integration."

Terminology	Definition	Example
Sensory Integration	*Sensory integration* is the overarching theory posed by Dr. Ayres in the 1970s to describe our ability to take information in from the environment and process, organize, and synthesize this input so as to formulate an adaptive response (Ayres, 1979) or effective plan of action.	**LaKeisha,** a 9-month-old baby, hears an airplane but does not know what she is hearing. She points to the airplane and looks at her mom as if to say, "What's that?" In this scenario, the baby hears the sound of the airplane, the sound registers in her brain, and her brain sends back a message saying, "point to mommy and look at her." If a child has trouble integrating information in this manner, she might cry, scream, look around but not actually locate the sound. She might even act out a combination of these maladaptive responses.
Sensory Integrative Dysfunction	*Sensory integrative dysfunction* refers to the brain's inability to effectively organize and process stimuli in a way that provides a person with accurate information about his environment (Ayres, 1979). If a person cannot accurately interpret information such as the honking of a horn, a gentle touch, or the whirring of a ceiling fan, this might not only impact his reaction and "behavior," but also negatively affect his emotions and learning.	**Roberto** was sitting in math class trying to pay attention, but he kept finding his eyes drift to the ceiling fan. He stared and stared until a loud voice interrupted his staring. "Roberto, what is the answer to number 3?" He looked around at the other children who were staring at him, realized he had missed critical pieces of information, and began to cry. In this situation, Roberto's learning and feelings were impacted by his inability to tune out the ceiling fan and focus on the math lesson.
Processing	*Processing* refers to the brain's ability to systematize and organize information in a meaningful way in order to respond appropriately and effectively to the situation at hand. Tracy Murnan Stackhouse, MA, OTR (personal conversation, May 28, 2008) discusses the duality that exists in sensory processing – the "high route" or praxis and the "low route" or modulation. All of these concepts will be discussed further in Chapter 1.	**Alejandro,** age 8, was sitting in the family room watching his favorite show when his babysitter told him to start getting ready so that they could go to the park. Alejandro just sat there. A couple of minutes later, the babysitter set Alejandro's shoes and socks in front of him and again asked him to get ready to go. Alejandro was excited to go to the park, but again he just sat there. Finally, the sitter began getting frustrated and told him that she would count to three and if had not put his shoes on, they would not be going. Alejandro stood up and threw his shoe across the room. "I can't put my shoes and socks on. I don't know how. I just can't do it." Alejandro yelled back. Just then, his mom walked in and explained to the sitter that Alejandro has difficulties with praxis and motor planning and needs help to put his shoes and socks on. It seemed Alejandro also had difficulty modulating his reactions both in the sensory realm as well as the emotional. These difficulties fall within the processing arena.

Terminology	Definition	Example
Praxis	*Praxis* is the ability to plan, organize, and sequence actions (Stackhouse, Graham, & Laschober, 2002). Praxis contributes to our ability to plan and carry out actions that are familiar or unfamiliar such as throwing a ball in the air, swinging a tennis racket, and hitting the ball in order to serve in tennis. Ayres referred to this as motor planning. When a person has trouble in this area, it is referred to as *dyspraxia* (Ayres, 1979).	*See previous example.*
Sensory Modulation or Sensory Regulation	*Sensory modulation* or *sensory regulation* are terms used to describe a person's response to the sensory input he experiences in the environment. The response to the input must be equal to the actual input (Stackhouse et al., 2002), such that a person's reaction should be "just right" rather than an over- or under-reaction. If a child experiences challenges in the area of sensory modulation, this may lead to sensory-seeking or sensory-avoiding behavior, sensory defensiveness, and difficulties with self-regulation (Stackhouse et al., 2002).	For example, if we walk into a restaurant and it smells fishy, we might note the fishy smell, maybe comment on it, and then move on. If we have trouble regulating our sensory reactions, we might smell the smell, jump up and down, yelling, "I can't eat here," and storm out.
Sensory Seeking	*Sensory seeking* describes a child's desire to expose himself to a particular form of sensory input.	Years ago, I worked with a very young child who could not stop smelling the candles around the house. His communication skills were delayed, and one of his first efforts to communicate was to ask for the candles (when they were not lit) so he could smell them. This activity seemed to calm his body and lower his level of arousal. It became apparent to us after awhile (and a lot of candles) that he learned better after he smelled the candles – his concentration increased, he seemed calmer and had less need to jump around the room. In this example, his seeking the smell of the candles gave him the input he needed to slow his body down and be able to learn.

Terminology	Definition	Example
Sensory Arousal	*Sensory arousal* describes the child's level of awareness and alertness in a given situation. Williams and Shellenberger (1996) developed a system of intervention that assists children (with adult support and training) to better understand their arousal level and better regulate their level of alertness by comparing their body to an engine. Williams and Shellenberger describe three levels of alertness or engine speed: high, low, and just right. The ability to regulate one's level of sensory arousal is referred to as *sensory regulation* or *modulation*.	Janie (age 12) always found herself moving too quickly in the wrong places. She could not seem to settle her body and sit still when her friends wanted to watch a movie. She found herself bouncing her legs, tapping her fingers, and generally fidgeting. Her fidgets inevitably drove her friends crazy. In this situation, Janie's arousal level did not match the task. She had trouble bringing her arousal level down to concentrate and watch the movie.
Emotional Modulation or Regulation	*Regulation* and *modulation* are also terms used in the emotional realm. *Emotional modulation* or *regulation* are terms used to describe the emotional response we have to different events and our ability to manage these emotions, for example, to feel sadness but be able to prevent the sad feelings from increasing in intensity to the point that we feel out of control. Of course, there are times when we do feel very strong emotions, such as from the death of a loved one, but most of the time, we are challenged to experience many different feelings throughout the day ranging from positive to negative, intense to mild, and we need to be able to experience these feelings and still function in our daily lives.	I have found it useful to think of feelings as the air in a balloon. If you have too little air (or helium) in a balloon, the balloon looks deflated and won't float. When we regulate our feelings, we are trying to make sure we have just the right amount of feeling in our balloons (or bodies) so that we feel just right. If we are unable to effectively regulate our feelings either because they grew too large too fast, or we had a particularly bad day, the feelings may grow too large, too intense and the "air" in the balloon would expand to the point that the balloon might POP! Remember Alejandro from above. Let's say he did not experience any of the above difficulties with motor planning and praxis. Perhaps he just didn't like being told what to do and had trouble transitioning away from the television. His inflated reaction of throwing his shoe may have been an example of an inability to modulate his emotions.

The above terminology will be expanded upon and explored throughout this workbook, particularly in Chapter 3, so that you can identify areas that come naturally for the child and areas that seem to pose challenges. By pinpointing areas that present challenges, you can begin to find more suitable interventions that will reduce the challenges while capitalizing on the child's the areas of strength.

Explorers:

I am guessing that you probably skipped reading the Introduction, and that is fine. It is important for you to know, though, that occupational therapists are the therapists who help people with sensory difficulties. In Chapter 3, you will get a chance to look through the different sensory systems and get to know your sensory self a bit better.

The good news is that the better you understand your sensory and emotional self, the better you will be able to learn and control your body. If you feel good about your learning and good about how well you control your body, you can feel good about yourself!!! If you feel like you want more help after you read this book, occupational therapy might be a good way to go. An adult, such as a parent, teacher, or mental health therapist, can help you find an occupational therapist to work with to continue what we have started here.

CHAPTER 1

THE PROCESS OF SENSORY INTEGRATION

Each person processes sensory information in his or her own way. Some people can focus on a task and ignore the other stimuli around them such as the whir of a ceiling fan or the sounds of traffic outside their window. Others are distracted by these stimuli to the point of being unable to complete the task at hand.

For example, as I sit here and attempt to describe sensory integration, the papers strewn all over my desk and piled next to me on the floor could interrupt my thoughts or simply fade into the background unnoticed. Thankfully, I am able to ignore the papers and go on with my writing, but for others, the papers could be so distracting that they would not be able to focus.

Sensory integration is a matter of filtering – it is the ability to filter in the relevant stimuli while simultaneously filtering out the irrelevant.

In addition to our ability to focus and concentrate, sensory input can also impact our moods – in both positive and negative ways. The smell of home-made cookies makes me feel calm and peaceful. On the other hand, if I am in a crowded place and people constantly bump into me (which is common since I am 5'1"), I become irritated and upset rather quickly. My body goes into overload. I want to escape the situation and if for some reason I am unable to get away, I may have a meltdown (at least on the inside) or demonstrate other extreme behavioral signs.

Unfortunately, schools often provide the perfect combination of sensory stimuli to create sensory overload. Think of what P.E. can be like. The child may or may not have to change clothes to participate, listen to the teacher's voice, which is usually loud and often echoes in such a large room, follow directions while moving around the room and in and out among other people, and try to ignore the other children's voices, which are probably loud and echoing, too. To add insult to injury, there are skill demands (such as catching and throwing a ball), rule demands (such as following the rules to a game), bright lights, and the smell of rubber or varnish, depending upon the type of flooring in the room. All of these examples of sensory stimuli could make a child feel overloaded. For some children, such overload causes them to be frustrated, sad, and/or angry.

The examples in school are endless – the cafeteria (echoing sounds, intense smells, noise, bright lights, taste of food), the classroom (lights, sound of the heater, children whispering, posters, noise in the hallway). Indeed, schools are a regular smorgasbord of sensory stimuli.

Our ability to tune in, tune out, filter, discriminate, and integrate information varies greatly depending on who we are, how we are feeling, how tired we are, how much we know, and how well our sensory system functions in general.

Smelling, hearing, touching, seeing, and tasting make each day an adventure. Young children are just beginning to identify and make meaning out of what they smell when they arrive at the zoo or a restaurant. They are beginning to discriminate the way soft, jiggling Jello feels in their mouths versus the way a crisp cookie does.

Sensory Difficulties

The ability to discriminate what we experience with our senses is a far more complicated process than is generally acknowledged since it is something that most of us do automatically and unconsciously. Dr. A. Jean Ayres likened our brain's ability to respond to the different sensations in our environment to a traffic officer. She talked about how the brain is typically able to sort, prioritize, organize, and respond to stimuli in a rather easy, seamless manner. However, at times, the brain is unable to respond to the sensations entering the brain, causing a "traffic jam" (Ayres, 1979, p. 47). To complicate matters, the way we react to our senses can vary depending upon the circumstances in our life. For example, if you have a sinus infection and plugged-up ears, you may react in a dramatically different way while listening to someone speak in a crowded room than when you are feeling well. You may find it extremely frustrating and upsetting to have trouble filtering pieces of a conversation because of the noise in the room, when this is normally a relatively easy task requiring little or no thought.

Because most people's sensory systems function smoothly much of the time, we often do not realize the havoc that can result when they do not. For example, what appears to be a child's totally unprovoked, out-of-the blue meltdown in circle time may have been provoked by sensory overload in gym class earlier in the day.

Often, people associate sensory difficulties with a specific disorder such as an autism spectrum disorder or attention deficit disorder, or with a diagnosis of sensory integrative dysfunction. Difficulties with sensory information can be present in many different children – whether specifically diagnosed or not. As mentioned earlier, there are many reasons for sensory issues, in addition to neurological difficulty. These include, but are not limited to, illness such as a cold, fatigue, or a sudden life change. Also, sensory issues can be more pronounced at times and less pronounced at others.

For these reasons, it is important to explore children's experiences from a sensory perspective. The more we look at what children are noticing through their eyes, ears, hands, mouths, and noses, the better we can facilitate more effective integration and discrimination of these stimuli. As Dr. Ayres noted, the information we receive through all places on our body is sent to our brain, which kicks out a message to our body. If the brain really was a traffic officer in the analogy of Dr. Ayres, the officer might make one of these three statements in response to a bad smell such as something burning. The statements would cause the person to either over-react, under-react, or react "just right."

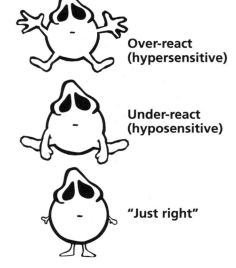

Over-react
(hypersensitive)

Under-react
(hyposensitive)

"Just right"

1. "Watch out! That is a disgusting smell – move quickly, scream, jump up and down, run!!!."

2. "Smell, I don't think there is anything there – no big deal. Just sit as still as you can. Keep your body quiet. No need to hurry."

3. "That smell tells me something burning. No need to panic, just walk over to the oven and turn it off. You'll need to take the tray out of the oven so don't forget a pot holder or you might get burned."

The messages sent from our brain cause us to act a certain way. They also cause us to **feel** a certain way. If our brain was telling us to scream, run, and move quickly in response to a bad smell, we may begin to feel agitated and frightened. If our brain tells us to shut our body down and remain still, we might begin to feel tired and anxious because being completely shut off may not feel good. However, if, as in the third scenario above, our brain gives us an action plan that is effective and assists us in reacting appropriately to a situation, we may feel more at ease even in a stressful situation.

If children are able to identify what makes their bodies over-react, under-react, and react "just right," they are in a better position to find and use strategies that help them engage in a "just right" reaction more often. It is my belief that the more children's bodies react in a helpful, effective way, the more they will feel positively about themselves, their peers, and the world around them. The more children can effectively allocate their sensory resources to all of the different aspects of their lives – relationships, school work, playing, listening, regulating emotions, and managing their environment – the more confident they will feel.

In the chart below, we see the clear difference between the brain's inability to effectively handle the stream of sensory input, versus the brain's successful management of sensory input. In "Closed for Renovation," the sensory information either (a) enters the brain accurately, resulting in an adaptive response; (b) is unable to reach the brain at all; or (c) reaches the brain and a maladaptive response is sent back to the body. The result is a choppy system that offers little to no appropriate adaptive responses. In "Open and Up and Running," on the other hand, the messages and responses flow smoothly, which results in clear, effective adaptive responses.

Closed for Renovation

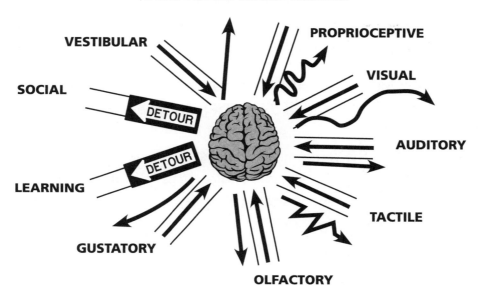

Open and Up and Running

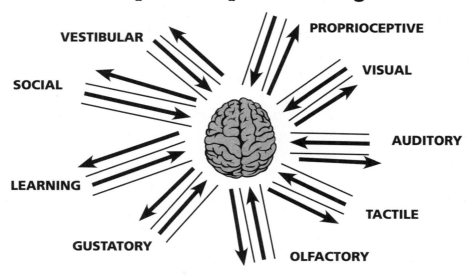

Sorting out Emotional and Sensory Regulation

For years, I have conducted home visits for very young children. Usually, I receive calls from speech/language pathologists, occupational therapists, early childhood educators, and case managers asking me to observe a child to help them determine whether sensory issues seem to be the driving factor behind the child's emotional responses, or whether it is the emotions that seem to be driving the sensory issues. For example, Johanna is a child who is constantly getting into trouble for hiding under the table in the housekeeping area of her classroom. The teachers have wondered if she is sad or having trouble interacting with her friends. As I observed her, it became apparent that we needed to rule out whether hiding under the table stems from emotions (sadness in social situations) or from a desire to sit in a small, confined area.

This is not an easy distinction to make. There are many clues to look for in making this determination such as whether a child is defensive to touch all of the time or just defensive to touch when he is experiencing heightened emotions. It also helps to be a "historian" and look at the sequence of events (if you have the full sequence) to try to sort out the initial triggers. We will explore this later in the book and discuss potential clues to unravel this challenging conundrum. Nevertheless, in the end, this mystery may remain challenging for most. It is important to keep the interactions between the emotional and sensory systems in mind as you read this book as it might help you refine and identify interventions that are most helpful.

CHAPTER 2

HOW OUR SENSORY SYSTEMS WORK

 Facilitators and 🔍 Explorers

Reasons for Developing a Better Understanding
of Sensory Integration

Sue left her language arts class and headed to science class. As she was walking through her middle school hallway, Fred yelled "hi" to her from across the crowd, two students accidentally bumped into her, and another student's backpack grazed the side of her shoulder. One of the lights in the ceiling was flickering.

Sue looked at her watch to make sure she had enough time to detour and stop at her locker. She quickened her pace as she turned left toward her locker. She tried her combination three times before she finally got her locker open. Just as she reached in for the book she needed, two kids next to her bumped each other, sending a book flying in her direction.

Sue picked up the book, which had something slimy on it and handed it back to them. She wiped her hand on her pants. Then she grabbed the book she needed from her locker, put it in her backpack, slammed the locker shut to the chorus of three other students closing their lockers, and finally resumed her journey toward science class.

On the way, she noticed a sign on the wall next to the cafeteria about the upcoming school dance, but she didn't have time to read it. Sue hurried through the hall with the strong odor of lunch filtering out of the cafeteria door. Finally, 2 ½ long minutes from the beginning of her journey, she put her backpack down with a clunk next to her chair and sat down in the cold seat in science class.

Sue's expedition from language arts to science class was filled with well over 10 different forms of sensory input. If Sue had trouble regulating any of the sensory input, this journey could be a nightmare for her. It may leave her arousal level too high (over-reactive) or too low (under-reactive). It might also cause her to feel overwhelmed and unable to focus in class.

This vignette illustrates how critical it is that we develop a better understanding of sensory systems and how they work. If we do not, a child like Sue may experience failure, distress, and "behavioral" issues that will more than likely interfere with her ability to feel successful in school (or in other areas of her life).

In this chapter, we will explore how our sensory systems work and take a look at the various components of our sensory systems. As mentioned in the Introduction, this book will use the term *sensory integration* for the sake of ease and clarity to describe our ability to take information in from the environment and subsequently process, organize, and synthesize it so as to formulate an adaptive response. *Sensory processing* is viewed here as a component under the sensory integration umbrella (see page

16), referring to the brain's ability to organize information in such a way that a person can respond with a systematic, effective motoric response (such as stop a ball when it is coming toward him), and keep his body regulated by reacting "just right" to stimuli rather than over- or under-reacting.

The following example illustrates how the olfactory and tactile stimuli of "Maggie's Breath" work their way through the central nervous system (CNS) so that an adaptive response might take place.

 Explorers: Check this out!

THE PROCESS OF ORGANIZING STIMULI INTO AN ADAPTIVE RESPONSE

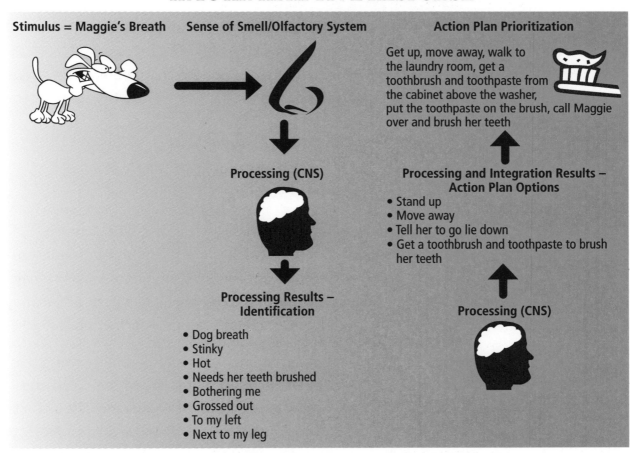

In the above diagram, the many steps that might take place when a stimulus impacts the olfactory and tactile systems are truncated into a few short steps. In reality, the processing or integration of these stimuli occur in split seconds in a person whose system of sensory integration is functioning well. However, for a person with sensory integrative dysfunction, this neurological process might look far more choppy and disorganized and might not provide an end response – walking away and brushing Maggie's teeth – that addresses the issue – the smell of stinky, hot doggy breath on your leg.

As you think about the process of organizing stimuli in the brain and body, it might help you think about how the child reacts to sensory input. Knowledge of the concepts involved in sensory integration will enable you, together with the child, to design strategies for coping with sensory challenges in the child's day-to-day life at home, at school, and in the community. Since most sensory problems do not just disappear, you are equipping the child with strategies for lifelong survival in the chaotic world of the senses.

To determine whether a particular area of sensory integration and/or systems is worth further exploration with a child, use the simple checklists provided on pages 133-136 as a starting point. Once you have determined whether or not the child seems to be struggling in a particular area, you can begin to add interventions to the toolbox page later in the book.

Sensory Processing

Sensory processing refers to the way in which our nervous system enables us to **perceive, integrate,** and **interpret** information that we are exposed to through our senses. This information may be internal or external. For example, our nervous system may perceive a headache and alert our body to take action to remedy it. As a result, we may rest or take medicine to feel better. This is an example of internal information.

Our nervous system may also pick up external sensations, such as someone touching our shoulder, and alert us to this information. Depending on the pressure of the touch and where it happens, it may be a friendly tap or gesture or a sign of aggression. If we don't know how to interpret this information, we may under-react and not be able to protect ourselves. Or conversely, we may over-react and accidentally turn someone away who was just trying to be helpful.

We need to be able to organize all of the different input we receive in our environment in order to adapt and respond effectively and appropriately. We also need to be able to prioritize information so that we can respond "just right." For example, a child sitting in a classroom during a lecture may have to be able to tune out the noise from the hallway, the heat in the room (since the air conditioner broke), and the fact that his legs are sticking to the chair, in order to hear the teacher and process the information she is imparting. If he cannot tune all those distractions out, he will miss critical information and be unable to complete the upcoming assignment. Effective sensory processing enables the child to prioritize the stimuli so that he can hear the teacher.

Most of the time, we are able to register information and process it in more or less a seamless manner:

The stimuli come in. Our nervous system processes them, filters out the irrelevant stimuli, and filters in the relevant stimuli.

At times, however, a difficulty in one or more of the sensory systems can cause problems and prevent accurate processing. In the above example, if the child had difficulties with his proprioceptive system (see the description in Chapter 3), he may not have been able to tune out the fact that his legs were sticking to the chair and would subsequently have missed the information in the lecture.

Motor Planning – Praxis

As mentioned in the Introduction, sensory processing can be divided into two parts – praxis and modulation. Praxis describes our ability to plan, organize, and carry out a particular action or series of actions. This is typically referred to as motor planning. In their book, *Asperger Syndrome and Sensory Issues* (2000), Myles, Cook, Miller, Rinner, and Robbins break motor planning into the following steps:

1. Coming up with an idea about the action

2. Having an accurate sense of where the body is

3. Starting the action

4. Executing the steps in the appropriate sequence

5. Making adjustments as needed

6. Knowing when to stop the action

Similarly, Stackhouse et al. (2002, p. 165) described the categories of praxis as identified by Ayres (1989) in her Sensory and Integration Praxis Tests.

1. Ideation, or the ability of the brain to conceive of an action: *What to do.*

2. Planning, or the ability to organize the plan for action: *How to do it.*

3. Execution, or the ability to carry out a sequence of action: *Just do it!*

Motor planning or praxis, then, involves a series of complicated steps completed in a split second so that a particular action or series of actions can be accomplished. At times, these actions are unconscious such as sitting on your suitcase, coordinating the direction and amount of your weight on the suitcase so that you can successfully close it after having stuffed it to overflowing. At other times, motor planning requires a more conscious "conversation" with ourselves such as when we are trying to remember the moves to a dance and need to talk ourselves through it as we go. Here is a great example.

Elizabeth, who is 1 year old, was sitting across from her sister, Samantha. Samantha reached over and tickled Elizabeth's toes a couple of times in a row, delighting in the giggles this produced in Elizabeth. After a while Samantha became distracted and moved to the other side of the room. Elizabeth watched Samantha go and then sat quietly for a couple of seconds. She slowly reached her hand toward her foot and tickled her own toes. Elizabeth smiled widely and tried it again. Samantha, in turn, became very excited to see Elizabeth imitate her, and this interaction soon became a game. This is a clear example of the ability to motor plan in order to imitate and recreate a novel action.

Dyspraxia

Some children have trouble organizing their bodies so that they can execute a movement or series of motions. This is referred to as dyspraxia (Ayres, 1979). Dyspraxia can affect children in a multitude of ways as they are unable to organize their actions in a meaningful, successful way. For example, in the above scenario, if Elizabeth was unable to recreate the toe tickle, any of the following things might have occurred:

She may have squeezed her toe too hard.

She may have fallen forward trying to reach for her foot.

She might have lost her balance and have fallen backward.

She probably would have become frustrated.

She would have missed out on a satisfying social interaction.

Sensory Modulation/Regulation

Sensory modulation is our ability to interpret and organize internal information (stomachache) and external information (the sound of hail) in an effective manner so that we react to the information in an even, relatively calm way ("just right"), rather than over- or under-react.

As illustrated in the diagram entitled Closed for Renovation on page 5, when sensory information flows into our central nervous system and adaptive messages flow out, we can keep our bodies in a "just right" state (Williams & Shellenberger, 1996).

To further illustrate sensory modulation, let's look at a typical school day for 9-year-old Ben.

Ben always misses the school bus. Every morning, he works very hard to get ready on time, but it is nearly impossible for him. His mom wakes him up ½ hour earlier so that he can get ready on time, but it hasn't worked. First, it takes five tries to get Ben to wake up and get out of bed. His mom and dad constantly tell him that he would have an easier time getting up if he went to bed earlier. For Ben, though, going to bed earlier has always been impossible. He lies, wide awake, legs swaying back and forth reading until long after his parents have gone to bed. His mom and dad argue about Ben's "defiance" around getting up; Ben feels badly about their arguing but he truly can't wake up. Ben's mom ends up driving him to school because he misses the bus – his brother always makes the high school bus (which is even earlier), but Ben just can't seem to get ready fast enough to make it to the bus.

Once Ben gets to school and is seated in class, things usually go from bad to worse – he cannot sit still. He can't seem to stop his feet from tapping. His teacher usually asks him to move to the back of the room (or worse, to the office) for disrupting the class with his tapping, pen twirling/dropping antics. Each school day brings a new adventure involving Ben trying to focus, concentrate, and attend, but consistently failing miserably. He's either in trouble for not responding to the teacher's questions and staring out of the window or in trouble for his one-man band performance with his pencil and feet. With each passing day, Ben feels more and more discouraged.

Ben's teachers, parents, and some of his friends are probably thinking Ben has a "behavior problem." They may be thinking that he just doesn't listen or care. However, if we investigate the situation further (perhaps with the help of an occupational therapist), we may find that Ben is having trouble regulating his body to meet the demands of the situation and needs assistance learning how to modulate his sensory system. Labeling him a "problem kid" and reacting in a behavioral way with consequences and rewards will probably do very little to ameliorate his difficulties. Providing Ben with sensory strategies that match his sensory struggles may do far more to increase his ability to regulate his body and thus improve his positive feelings of himself.

Sensory Defensiveness

Some people who have difficulties with sensory modulation may have what the literature (Ayres, 1979; Wilbarger & Wilbarger, 1991; Williams & Shellenberger, 1996) calls *sensory defensiveness*. A defensive reaction often occurs in the tactile sense but can occur in the other sensory systems. An example of olfactory and tactile defensiveness is as follows.

Fred walks into the gymnasium for a school assembly. The air conditioning isn't turned on yet since it is only April, but it is unseasonably warm. As a result, the gymnasium is hot, and Fred soon feel likes he is suffocating. The smell from the rubber floor is very strong to him. He starts to pull at the sleeves and neckline of his shirt and begins to jump around as the students stand waiting for their seats. His jumping sends him slamming into his friend Joe, causing both of them to fall to the ground.

In this situation, Fred over-reacted to the heat and smells in the room, as he could not modulate the sensory input. Rather than his brain organizing the heat sensation and the smell of rubber so that he could push his sleeves up and begin to ignore the smell, his brain sent a maladaptive response and told him to jump around (which, of course, would make him warmer in the long run and cause him to breath the smell in more rapidly).

The next section will provide you with the opportunity to explore sensory defensiveness further so that you can determine whether or not this seems to be an area of difficulty for the child. Sensory defensiveness is typically an area of difficulty for people who are hypersensitive (over-reactive) to stimuli.

Sensory Integration

Sensory integration refers to the ability to take in the information in the environment (and from our own bodies), synthesize it so that it makes sense, and then formulate a plan of action. In their book, *Asperger Syndrome and Sensory Issues: Practical Solutions for Making Sense of the World* (2000), Myles et al. describe the very complex process of being able to register, orient, interpret, organize, and execute a response to incoming stimuli in a simple, easy-to-understand way. Our ability to successfully get through the above five steps and integrate stimuli impacts what we do and say, and can ultimately affect the way we feel.

Thinking back to the earlier example of Sue walking through the hallway at school, sensory integration in that scenario refers to the process of Sue registering, interpreting, organizing, and executing a response to the noise, physical contact with others, lights, smells, her internal worry over time, and the burden of a heavy backpack.

If a child manages all of these stimuli well and can integrate them successfully, she will arrive to class ready to focus and listen – adaptive responses. If the child has trouble with this process of sensory integration, on the other hand, she may become aggressive on the way to class, experience intense emotions, have difficulty interacting with peers, and/or have trouble focusing in class. Thus, in order to effectively help this child, one must have a better understanding of all of the components of our sensory world. Sensory integration, sensory processing, and sensory systems will be explored in more detail in the next chapter.

Explorers: Check this out!

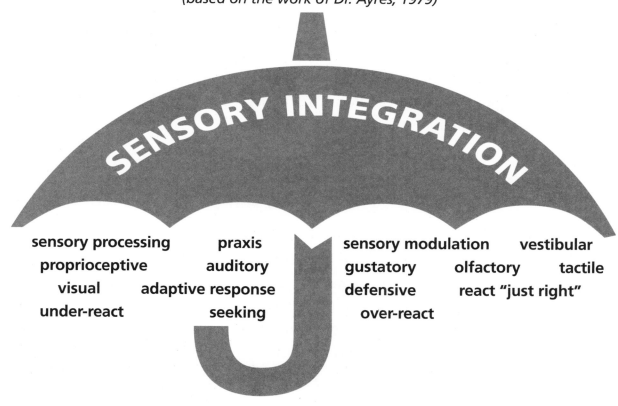

Sensory Integration Umbrella
(based on the work of Dr. Ayres, 1979)

sensory processing	praxis	sensory modulation	vestibular
proprioceptive	auditory	gustatory	olfactory	tactile
visual	adaptive response	defensive	react "just right"
under-react	seeking	over-react	

The following books contain helpful overviews of the sensory systems: *Asperger Syndrome and Sensory Issues – Practical Solutions for Making Sense of the World* (Myles et al., 2000), *The Out-of-Sync Child: Recognizing and Coping with Sensory Integration Dysfunction* (Kranowitz, 1998), *How Does Your Engine Run® A Leader's Guide to the Alert Program® for Self-Regulation* (Williams & Shellenberger, 1996), and *Sensory Integration and the Child* (Ayres, 1979).

As you read the next chapter, which provides an overview of our sensory systems, remember Ayres' concept of a traffic officer. Some children's brains send a message to over-react, some send a message to under-react, and some send the signal to react "just right."

HYPER- VERSUS HYPOSENSITIVE

Hypersensitive refers to a child who has a more dramatic reaction to even the smallest stimuli. A whisper might sound like a yell. A gentle touch might feel like a punch. *Hyposensitive,* on the other hand, refers to a child who reacts in a milder way than one might expect. For example, the child who is hyposensitive may underreact to stimuli that are quite intense to others. A yell might sound like a whisper. A punch may feel like a gentle touch.

Hypersensitivity and hyposensitivity pose their own challenges and benefits.

A child who is hypersensitive to stimuli may hear things before others become aware of them, which may offer advanced warning of a dangerous situation. He may also recognize pain or a painful situation sooner, which may prevent further harm. Additionally, he may realize the need to escape or leave a difficult situation more rapidly. On the other hand, a child who is more hypersensitive to stimuli may be highly reactive and have a difficult time concentrating or managing emotions as the intensity of the stimuli may generate intense and unmanageable feelings and responses.

A child who is hyposensitive to stimuli may end up in more dangerous situations more often. She may not realize the impact she has on others and may hurt somebody unintentionally. A child who is hyposensitive may remain in a situation that could be harmful for a longer period of time (such as playing in the snow even though her shoes are soaked through) as she may not feel the discomfort the cold is causing. Conversely, a child who is hyposensitive may be able to tune out noxious stimuli for a longer period of time, thus delaying an emotional or physical response to escape or move away.

To help determine whether the child tends to be more hypersensitive versus hyposensitive, please refer *Sensory Defensiveness and Under-Responsiveness* in Chapter 3.

CHAPTER 3

OVERVIEW OF OUR SENSORY SYSTEMS

Our sensory systems include the tactile, vestibular, proprioceptive, visual, auditory, gustatory, and olfactory systems. As illustrated in Table 3.1, the tactile system gives us information about qualities such as shape, texture, density, as well as warning signs of pain or pleasure. The vestibular system allows us to know where our bodies are in relation to objects or other people. This system also assists us in determining such things as the speed and movement of things around us. The proprioceptive system helps us be aware of sensations in our body parts and helps us use them effectively and efficiently. The visual system gives us information that enables us to move more effectively through space. The auditory system helps us determine where sounds are coming from, what the sounds are, and the qualities of these sounds such as loud or soft. The gustatory system is responsible for helping us distinguish tastes. Finally, the olfactory system allows us to determine the characteristics of different smells.

Table 3.1 Location and Functions of the Sensory Systems		
System	**Location**	**Function**
Tactile (touch)	**Skin** – density of cell distribution varies through-out the body. Areas of greatest density include mouth, hands, and genitals.	Provides information about the environment and object qualities (touch, pressure, texture, hard, soft, sharp, dull, heat, cold, pain).
Vestibular (balance)	**Inner ear** – stimulated by head movements and input from other senses, especially visual.	Provides information about where our body is in space, and whether or not we or our surroundings are moving. Tells about speed and direction of movement.
Proprioception (body awareness)	**Muscles and joints** – activated by muscle contractions and movement.	Provides information about where a certain body part is and how it is moving.
Visual (sight)	**Retina of the eye** – stimulated by light.	Provides information about ob-jects and persons. Helps us define boundaries as we move through time and space.
Auditory (hearing)	**Inner ear** – stimulated by air/sound waves.	Provides information about sounds in the environment (loud, soft, high, low, near, far).
Gustatory (taste)	**Chemical receptors in the tongue** – closely en-twined with the olfactory (smell) system.	Provides information about dif-ferent types of taste (sweet, sour, bitter, salty, spicy).
Olfactory (smell)	**Chemical receptors in the nasal structure** – close-ly associated with the gustatory system.	Provides information about dif-ferent types of smell (musty, acrid, putrid, flowery, pungent).

From: *Asperger Syndrome and Sensory Issues – Practical Solutions for Making Sense of the World* by B. S. Myles, K. T. Cook, N. E. Miller, L. Rinner, and L. A. Robbins, 2000, Shawnee Mission, KS: Autism Asperger Publishing Company. Used with permission.

The descriptions of all of the sensory systems will be expanded upon in the next section so that you can begin to identify areas of challenge and areas of strength for the child (or yourself). We will also revisit sensory modulation and sensory defensiveness in more detail, as a basic understanding of these areas is critical for helping children process and respond to sensory information.

Sensory Systems and Possible Interventions

In presenting interventions throughout this book, I recognize that finding interventions that work for individual children is sometimes a process of trial and error. That is, children, and people in general, may react differently to different things despite being identified as having similar characteristics. In other words, despite the fact that two people are diagnosed with the same (or relatively same) areas of difficulty, they may respond very differently to interventions.

For example, Miguel and Ryan were both identified as needing interventions to assist them with their vestibular systems. Miguel seemed to have more difficulty after swinging on swings, while jumping and hopping helped him tremendously. Ryan, on the other hand, became out of control if he did a lot of games that involved jumping and hopping, yet he seemed far calmer after swinging.

I recommend approaching interventions in an investigative way. Try things and see what happens. Unfortunately, there is no one-size-fits-all intervention, even for two children with similar needs, and what works one day may not work the next. Children have good days and bad days as we all do. The areas of difficulty the child is experiencing may look different on different days. Finally, it is important to realize that it can take weeks to really see an improvement. So keep your toolbox of intervention strategies handy. You never know when you'll need it.

Intervention Challenge

The interventions described throughout this section are based on 12 years of reading texts and articles, observing occupational therapists and other professionals, and my own trial and error. The challenge I have is remembering which interventions are from where. I want to specifically recognize the following sources for their contributions to these interventions as well as thank all of the wonderful occupational therapists I have had the opportunity to observe throughout the years.

Buron, K. D., & Curtis, M. (2004). *The incredible 5-point scale: Assisting students with autism spectrum disorders in understanding social interactions and controlling their emotional responses.* Shawnee Mission, KS: Autism Asperger Publishing Company.

Gray, C. (1993). *The original Social Story™ book.* Arlington, TX: Future Horizons.

Kranowitz, C. S. (1998). *The out-of-sync child: Recognizing and coping with sensory integration dysfunction.* New York: Skylight Press.

Kranowitz, C. S. (2003). *The out-of-sync child has fun: Activities for kids with sensory processing disorder.* New York: Penguin Group Inc.

Myles, B. S., Cook, K. T., Miller, N. E., Rinner, L., & Robbins, L. A. (2000). *Asperger Syndrome and sensory issues: Practical solutions for making sense of the world.* Shawnee Mission, KS: Autism Asperger Publishing Company.

Williams, M. S., & Shellenberger, S. (1996). *"How does your engine run?"® A leader's guide to the Alert Program® for self-regulation.* Albuquerque, NM: TherapyWorks.

Facilitators and Explorers

 **Auditory System**

Your auditory system detects sounds and assists you in determining the pitch and volume of sound, as well as the distance of the sound from where you are. Each person can hear sounds differently, depending on the way in which their auditory sense is functioning and the way in which the sounds are processed. The auditory system protects us from entering situations that could be harmful to us. For example, the sound of a siren signals a firetruck is coming, to stop us from stepping out into the traffic.

Areas to Observe Related to the Auditory System
(Check off the areas that apply to the child)

☐ Does the child cover his/her ears a lot?

☐ Does the child seem to shy away from loud sounds?

☐ Does the child verbalize concerns regarding noises?

☐ Does the child seem to notice sounds others don't notice (such as the ticking of a clock or the hum of fluorescent lights)?

Interventions for Addressing Challenges with the Auditory System

• Create a Social Story™ (Gray, 1993) (see Appendix, page 130).

• Have the child use headphones.

• Have the child put a piece of cotton in his/her ears.

• Decrease time spent in loud areas.

• Allow the child to avoid places that echo, such as the cafeteria.

• Teach the child a number system to help create a better understanding of the volume of sounds (Buron & Curtis, 2004; see Appendix, page 131).

• Have the child sit in the front of the classroom or to one side of the room. (Some children hear better out of one ear than the other. If you suspect this is the case, you may want to seek a consultation with an audiologist.)

• Play a game in which the child works on identifying different sounds in the environment.

• Play the above game but hide in different places in the room and have the child attempt to identify the location of the sound you are making.

• Put different items in containers, shake them, and have the child identify what is inside by the sound it is making (Kranowitz, 2003).

Areas to Observe Related to My Auditory System
(Check off the areas that apply to you)

☐ Do I cover my ears a lot?

☐ Do I tend to avoid loud sounds?

☐ Do I find myself talking a lot about noises?

☐ Do I seem to notice sounds others don't notice (such as the ticking of a clock or the hum of fluorescent lights)?

Interventions for Addressing Challenges with My Auditory System

- Ask someone you trust such as your teacher, mom, dad, or therapist to help you create a Social Story™. (You can look in the Appendix on page 130 for more information.)

- Use headphones to block out noise in loud situations. Make sure you ask your teacher, parents, or therapist if it is an appropriate time to use them.

- Carry cotton balls or ear plugs with you (you can find ear plugs that let some of the sound in and others that drown more of the sound out). Put them in your ears to help you manage the sound. Again, be sure to ask your parents, teachers, or therapist if it is an appropriate time to use them.

- If possible, decrease the amount of time you spend in loud places.

- If possible, stay away from places that echo as they may be harder for you. If you can't avoid it, then remember your ear plugs.

- Learn a number system to help you monitor sound volume as well as your own voice volume. (You can look at page 131 in the Appendix for more information.)

- Did you know that you may hear better out of one ear than another, or that you may be able to focus better in class depending upon where you sit in class? Ask your teacher for help figuring this out.

- There are some fun games you can play with your parents, teachers, or therapist to work on strengthening your auditory system (see page 22).

Visual System

The visual system provides information regarding items, people, distance, light and dark, etc. This system also helps us determine our position in space as well as gather other information about our environment. For many people on the autism spectrum, the visual system is a strength. The visual system assists us with identifying things that may be harmful to us in our environment.

Areas to Observe Related to the Visual System
(Check off the areas that apply to the child)

☐ Does the child hold things at odd angles to his/her eyes?

☐ Does the child move his face very close to an object when looking at it?

☐ Does the child seem to notice a light that is flickering when others don't notice it?

☐ Does the child seem to be distracted by posters and other items on the wall to the point that it interrupts his/her ability to work?

☐ Does the child seem to do better if you reduce the visual field (e.g., 10 math problems on a page versus 20)?

Interventions for Addressing Challenges with the Visual System

• Turn fluorescent lights off, when possible, and use regular light bulbs.

• Reduce the visual field as described above or by placing a piece of plain paper on half of the page so that the child can focus on part of the page at a time.

• Play games that include gesturing and visual information and eliminate auditory information, such as variations of "Simon Says" or *Charades*.

• Help the child recognize when items in the visual field are pulling him off task.

• Have the child sit at the front of the classroom to eliminate some of the visual distractions.

Areas to Observe Related to My Visual System
(Check off the areas that apply to you)

☐ Do people comment that I am holding things near my eyes in a funny way?

☐ Do people comment that I hold objects very close to my face?

☐ Do I notice lights that are flickering when others don't seem to notice them?

☐ Do I find myself distracted by posters and other items on the wall to the point that I have trouble working?

☐ Do I do better if someone gives me less to focus on on a page?

Interventions for Addressing Challenges with My Visual System

• Work with your family, teachers, etc., to turn fluorescent lights off when possible, and use regular light bulbs.

• Make worksheets and other materials easier to look at and understand by putting a plain piece of paper on half of the page so you are only looking at half of the information at a time.

• Challenge yourself to watch television with the sound off and try to guess what is happening.

• Try to notice when things in your environment such as posters and artwork are pulling you off task and making it difficult to concentrate.

• With permission from your teacher, experiment with different seats in the classroom to see which one helps you focus the best.

Gustatory System

The gustatory system refers to the ability to taste things. This sense helps discriminate between sweet, salty, tart, sour, spicy, or mild. The gustatory system assists you with determining whether the food is safe to eat, and plays a role in determining the texture of foods. The gustatory system works closely with the olfactory system. The gustatory system can protect us from eating something that could harm us.

Areas to Observe Related to the Gustatory System
(Check off the areas that apply to the child)

☐ Does the child seem to be very particular about what she will eat (such as food of a certain texture)?

☐ Does the child gag easily?

☐ Does the child seem to have a strong reaction to seemingly mild tastes?

☐ Does the child seem to have a very high tolerance for spicy foods?

Interventions for Addressing Challenges with the Gustatory System

- Stimulate the mouth with an electric toothbrush.
- Slowly introduce new textures with very small bites.
- Offer multiple tries for a particular food. (It can take 15-20 repetitions to like a new food.)
- Massage around the child's mouth.
- Make a list of 5 to 10 foods and give the child the chance to pick a new food from the list to try each day or week.
- Consult with a specialist at your local Feeding and Swallowing Program.

Areas to Observe Related to My Gustatory System
(Check off the areas that apply to you)

☐ Is it hard for me to eat certain textures?

☐ Do I gag easily?

☐ Do some tastes really bother me more than other people who are eating the same thing?

☐ Do people comment on how I can eat things that are really spicy?

Interventions for Addressing Challenges with My Gustatory System

- Use an electric toothbrush to stimulate your mouth.
- Pick one new food to try each month. Take a small bite and see how it goes. If you feel comfortable, try taking a couple of bites of the new food. (Remember, it can take 15-20 repetitions to like a new food.)
- It is sometimes helpful to massage around your mouth. This may feel a bit strange and is something to do in a private place and not at school. Talk to your parents about it.

 *Tactile System*

The tactile system allows us to recognize and interpret touch sensations such as soft and hard, pain and pleasure. This system also helps identify pressure, temperature, and texture. We often think of our tactile system as only involving our hands, but it encompasses the entire surface of our body, including our arms, legs, and feet. The tactile system can protect us from harm as it alerts us if something is too hot or too cold, and thus could cause pain.

Areas to Observe Related to the Tactile System
(Check off the areas that apply to the child)

- ☐ Does the child seem to pull away from touch?
- ☐ Does the child seem to move herself into positions in which she is touching others?
- ☐ Does the child seem to have a particularly high threshold for pain? (e.g., falls down pretty hard but does not seem to be hurt)
- ☐ Does the child seem to have a particularly low threshold for pain? (e.g., gently bumps something and cries hard)
- ☐ Does the child seem to avoid touching certain textures?
- ☐ Does the child insist on washing hands immediately after touching certain textures such as paint or play dough?

Interventions for Addressing Challenges with the Tactile System

- Slowly introduce different textures to the child, reassuring him that he can wash his hands if the texture feels uncomfortable on his hands. These might include, but are not limited to, finger paints, sand, marshmallow, and "goop." (Goop is similar in consistency to slime. You can find a recipe for goop at the following website: http://www.placeofourown.net/activity.php?id=199)

- Warn the child ahead of time if you are going to touch her.

- Let the child choose clothing with textures that will feel okay to him.

- Create clear time boundaries around things like brushing teeth or hair by saying "count to 20" and then it will be done.

- Buy Therapuddy and let the child play with it. (Therapuddy, also called "exercise putty," may be found at www.youcantoocan.com, or "fitness putty," found at www.sammonspreston.com)

- Massage lotion into the child's hands.

- Play a game in which you put different items into empty cans (coffee cans, baby formula cans) and ask the child to reach into the can to identify what a given item is by touching it. You can use such items as uncooked pasta, cooked spaghetti noodles, beads, cotton balls, and sponges.

Areas to Observe Related to My Tactile System
(Check off the areas that apply to you)

☐ Is it hard for me to tolerate other people touching me?

☐ Do people ask me to move out of their space because I am touching them?

☐ Do I have a really high threshold for pain? (It takes a lot for me to feel pain)

☐ Do I have a really low threshold for pain? (I feel pain very quickly)

☐ Do I find myself avoiding certain textures such as sand, grass, paint, slimy foods?

☐ Do I feel like I have to wash my hands immediately after touching something like sand, paint, or slimy food?

Interventions for Addressing Challenges with My Tactile System

- Write a list of textures that are hard for you to touch such as sand, finger paints, and marshmallow. Pick one new texture to get used to each month and ask your mom or therapist to help you get it. Set aside some time to work with the texture to see if you can tolerate touching it. You might want to do this at a time when you will have lots of relaxation time if you feel stressed after touching it. You can even challenge yourself to make goop (by yourself or with the help of an adult). You can find a recipe for goop at the following website: http://www.placeofourown.net/activity.php?id-199.

- Try to identify people with whom you interact who tend to touch you on the shoulder, arm, back more than others. This might help to prepare you so that you can try to control your reaction when they do touch you.

- You may already be doing this, but try to wear clothing that is comfortable for you. With a parents' help, cut out the tags.

- Help yourself with things like brushing your teeth or your hair by telling yourself to count to 20. Counting will not only be a nice distraction, it will also highlight how quickly these tasks are over.

- Ask an adult to help you find and buy Therapuddy. Therapuddy, which is also called "exercise puddy," maybe found at www.youcantoocan.com, or "fitness puddy" at www.sammonspreston.com. You can keep the puddy in your backpack or in some other a place where you can easily access it so you can squeeze it if you are beginning to feel like you want to fidget or are having trouble concentrating. Squeezing might help you feel calmer and concentrate better.

- There are some fun games you can play (with an adult) to assist you in the tactile area. One such game may be found on page 28.

Olfactory System

The olfactory system is responsible for giving you information about the odors in your environment. This might include the sweet smell of a flower or the foul smell of curdled milk. The olfactory system provides protection in the sense that it enables us to detect a smell that could be dangerous to us such as gas from a gas leak.

Areas to Observe Related to the Olfactory System
(Check off the areas that apply to the child)

☐ Does the child smell things repetitively?

☐ Does the child seem to notice smells that are difficult for others to perceive?

☐ Does the child seem particularly sensitive to smells to the point that she becomes distressed when she notices them?

☐ Does the child seem to have difficulty identifying and discriminating between smells?

☐ Does the child lick things that aren't appropriate to lick?

☐ Does the child gag frequently?

Interventions for Addressing Challenges with the Olfactory System

- Play a game where the child tries to identify different smells in his environment.

- Have the child chew gum to distract from smells.

- Count to see how long it takes for the smell to fade to the point that the child doesn't notice it any more.

- Have the child suck on a mint to distract from the smell.

- Slowly introduce new smells to the child. You can do this by buying a few candles to smell or by going through your spice rack. You can make this into a game.

Areas to Observe Related to My Olfactory System
(Check off the areas that apply to you)

☐ Do people comment on my holding things up to my nose to smell them a lot?

☐ Do I notice smells that others do not seem to notice?

☐ Do a lot of smells really bother me?

☐ Is it hard for me to determine what I am smelling?

☐ Have I gotten in trouble (or tried to avoid getting in trouble) for licking something I wasn't supposed to lick?

☐ Do I gag a lot?

Interventions for Addressing Challenges with My Olfactory System

• Play a game with yourself and try to identify the different smells in the environment. If you want to check to see if you are right, you can ask a familiar adult (parent, teacher, therapist) their opinion. (Remember: Don't ask a teacher in the middle of class as it will disrupt the class.)

• Chew gum to distract yourself from smells.

• Count to see how long it takes for a certain smell to fade to the point that you don't notice it any more.

• Suck on a mint to distract yourself from the smell.

• Experiment with smelling different smells such as those in a candle store to see whether or not you like them.

Vestibular System

This is the sensory system that responds to motion or changes of head movement. Perception of movement, gravity, development of balance, equilibrium, body control, and muscles are all part of the vestibular system. This system is also important to consider in connection with bilateral coordination (coordination between both sides of the body), development of hand dominance (use of one hand for tasks; i.e., right- or left-handed), and perception of right/left direction.

Areas to Observe Related to the Vestibular System
(Check off the areas that apply to the child)

☐ Is the child using one hand for most tasks?

☐ Does the child seem like a "bull in a china shop" when moving through space?

☐ Can the child imitate motor movements?

☐ Is the child able to balance on playground equipment?

☐ Does the child fall down a lot?

Areas to Observe Related to My Vestibular System
(Check off the areas that apply to you)

☐ Do I use one hand for most tasks?

☐ Do I bump into a lot of things by accident? (Do people sometimes say I'm like a bull in a china shop?)

☐ Can I imitate motor movements such as if someone tries to teach me a new dance or a new move in sports?

☐ Can I, or was I able to balance on playground equipment?

☐ Do I trip or fall down a lot?

Interventions for Addressing Challenges with My Vestibular System

• Playing on swings

• Going down slides

• Riding on merry-go-rounds

• Playing on a "sit-n-spin" toy

- Riding a tricycle
- Playing jumping or hopping games
- Rolling across the floor
- Rocking in a chair
- Playing on a teeter-totter
- Rolling inside a play tunnel or barrel

Proprioceptive System

This system includes awareness of one's body in space as well as awareness of sensations coming from joints, muscles, and tendons. As a result, proprioceptive input contributes to an awareness of posture and movement. This system also contributes to developing the ability to sequence movements and organize them in a coordinated manner. This is particularly important when trying to complete motor tasks such as sports activities, moving through a crowded space, riding a bike, doing jumping jacks, skipping, and tying shoes.

One of the most difficult times of the school day for a child with proprioceptive difficulties is P.E. The coordination involved in playing kickball, for example, can be daunting. The child has to learn to organize running up to the ball, kicking it, and then running to first base. This coordination may be nearly impossible without intervention, such as running obstacle courses or engaging in activities that provide proprioceptive input, including jumping, running, or carrying heavy things.

The proprioceptive and vestibular systems also work in combination with other parts of our sensory system. For example, the proprioceptive system in combination with our sense of touch is often referred to as the somatosensory system. The somatosensory system describes the perception of touch and the awareness of one's body in space at the same time. In other words, the sense of touch encompasses a larger ability to determine such things as temperature, pain, texture, and shape. This system is very important for such tasks as picking up a bottle of juice, carrying things of different weights, holding a marker, and lifting a fork full of food to your mouth.

Areas to Observe Related to the Proprioceptive System
(Check the areas that apply to the child)

☐ Is the child bumping into things or people a lot? (sensory seeking)

☐ Is the child able to coordinate movements such as dancing, singing songs, riding a bicycle?

☐ Is the child "in other people's space" a lot?

☐ Does the child seem to have a limited concept of others' personal space?

☐ Can the child imitate motor tasks? (playing such games as "Simon Says," imitating cooking in the play kitchen)

Areas to Observe Related to My Proprioceptive System
(Check off the areas that apply to you)

☐ Does it feel good when I bump into people or things?

☐ Was it, or is it still hard for me to dance, ride a bicycle?

☐ Do people tell me I am in their "space" a lot?

☐ Is it hard for me to understand what "personal space" really means?

☐ Was it, or is it hard for me to play "Simon Says," or imitate what other people are doing with their bodies?

Interventions for Addressing Challenges with the Proprioceptive System

- Jumping on a trampoline
- Hanging from monkey bars
- Wearing a weighted vest
- Sleeping with a weighted blanket
- Throwing and catching a heavy ball or bean bag
- Pressing hand prints into clay or play dough
- Rolling up tightly in a blanket
- Carrying chairs or other heavy objects
- Wringing out washcloths, hand towels, or sponges
- Two people lying on their backs opposite each other with the bottoms of their feet touching and pushing each other's feet
- Digging in heavy sand
- Sucking on a water bottle
- Chewing heavy or crunchy foods
- Bouncing on a ball

Sensory Modulation

Sensory modulation refers to the instinctive ability of the nervous system to determine the relevance of incoming sensory stimuli and either attend to them or tune them out as needed to be able to focus attention and process information in a meaningful way. For example, as I type this sentence, I hear a dog barking in the distance. My nervous system needs to block out the barking in order for me to be able to continue to attend to and type out my ideas. This is happening somewhat automatically for me at this moment, but that may not be the case for others in the same situation. Also, if I was feeling stressed over other matters or had a headache, I might not be able to tune out the barking.

Another example is the difficulty many children have of tuning out the noise in the school hallway during class so that they can attend to the teacher. An inability to modulate can lead to frustration, anger, or sadness as it may inhibit a person from being able to attend to and complete the task at hand.

Areas to Observe Related to Sensory Modulation
(Check the areas that apply to the child)

☐ Does the child seem to require a lot of repetition of information?
☐ Does the child seem unfocused?
☐ Does the child take excessive risks?
☐ Is the child "on the go" a lot of the time?
☐ Does the child cover his ears?
☐ Is the child easily agitated in crowds?

Interventions for Addressing Challenges with Sensory Modulation

- Have the child use headphones.
- Eliminate distractions.
- Improve external organization, such as how much information is on the walls, on the tables, etc.
- Clearly define work space.
- Have the child put cotton in her ears.
- Seat the child toward the front of the classroom so that there are fewer stimuli between the child and the teacher/board.
- Allow frequent breaks.
- Have the child practice over- and under-reacting and "just right" through role-plays.

Areas to Observe Related Sensory Modulation
(Check off the areas that apply to you)

☐ Do I need information repeated to me a lot?

☐ Is it hard for me to focus?

☐ Do I take a lot of risks?

☐ Am I always "on the go"?

☐ Do I cover my ears a lot?

☐ Do crowds make me feel uncomfortable?

Interventions for Addressing Challenges with Sensory Modulation

• Try using headphones.

• Eliminate distractions.

• Ask your teacher if distracting information and other materials can be removed from the classroom walls and tables.

• Clearly define your work space.

• Put cotton in your ears.

• Work with the teacher to sit in the front of the classroom to eliminate some of the sensory input. Your parents might be able to help you uncover situations at home or in public that feel too overwhelming for you. Together, you can work to think if strategies to manage or eliminate some of the input.

• Ask the teacher if you can take breaks.

• Try to notice when you are over-reacting to something, under-reacting, or reacting "just right." Once you have taken the time to pay attention to this, you can prepare yourself for the challenging situations so that you can maintain a "just right" reaction. An adult might be able to help you keep track of this and design strategies that might help you. The situations in which you feel "just right" may provide you with some clues about what's helpful and what's not. For example, perhaps you tend to react and feel "just right" when: the lighting is dim, you are playing a video game, you are chewing gum or you are listening to music. You might be able to use some of these things in situations that cause you to over-react or under-react.

Sensory Defensiveness and Under-Responsiveness

As we discussed in Chapter 2, some children are hypersensitive and thus tend to over-react to stimuli and others are hyposensitive and thus tend to under-react. Now that you have explored the different sensory systems and identified areas in which the child seems to experience difficulties, let's examine whether the child is typically hypo- or hypersensitive to stimuli.

Please keep in mind that the child may be hypersensitive in some areas and hyposensitive in others.

Sensory Defensiveness

"Sensory defensiveness or hypersensitivity stems from a dysfunction in the nervous system such that there is such difficulty regulating and filtering stimuli that the child becomes defensive to all stimuli" (Kranowitz, 1998, p. 57).

Hypersensitivity is often referred to as sensory defensiveness. Sensory defensiveness describes what appears to be an exaggerated response to typical sensations. For example, I tend to touch children to comfort them when I work with them. This may be a gentle touch on the shoulder meant to reassure or a high-five to provide praise. For children who are defensive to touch, rather than providing reassurance or praise, such touching may have the opposite effect, causing anger or discomfort. Similarly, children who experience sensory defensiveness in the olfactory (smell) sense may notice odors that those around them are not able to smell. The last time I got new the carpet in my office, the children with whom I work who are sensory defensive noticed the "new-carpet smell" long after anyone else paid any attention to it.

Areas to Observe Related to Sensory Defensiveness (Hypersensitivity)
(Check the areas that apply to the child)

☐ Does the child typically pull away from touch?

☐ Does the child get agitated in crowds?

☐ Does the child misperceive touch?

☐ Does the child react strongly to seemingly mild smells?

Interventions for Addressing Challenges with Sensory Defensiveness (Hypersensitivity)

• Give input in anticipation of difficult environments.

• Be alert to stimulation in the environment and help the child understand and deal with it.

• Be aware of the child's threshold and remove him before the stimuli become too overwhelming.

Areas to Observe Related to Sensory Defensiveness (Hypersensitivity)
(Check the areas that apply to you)

☐ Does touch bother me to the point that I tend to pull away from it?

☐ Do a lot of people in one space bother me?

☐ Does touch often feel uncomfortable to me (such as a teacher putting a hand on my shoulder)?

☐ Do smells bother me a lot?

Interventions for Addressing Challenges with Sensory Defensiveness (Hypersensitivity)

• Ask an occupational therapist or adult to help you determine what "input" helps you the most and how to get that input. Input means information you give to your brain to increase your ability to respond "just right" to situations. This may include deep pressure on your shoulders, chewing something hard or crunchy, or doing something active such as jumping before a challenging situation. If you will be entering a difficult environment, give yourself that input (or ask someone to help you get it) ahead of time.

• Take inventory of the stimuli in your environment (we will explore the meaning of stimuli later in this book but for now, remember stimuli means something that CAUSES you to think or feel a certain way). Try to recognize stimuli that might cause you to over-react so that you can either avoid it or remind yourself to stay calm.

• Know your limits – know when you are beginning to have trouble and need to leave a situation.

Under-Responsiveness

I am referring to children who are hyposensitive as being "under-responsive" to stimuli. Children who tend to be hyposensitive to stimuli appear to be oblivious to certain types of input. These children may fall down and not feel intense pain despite the fact that they bruised their knee pretty badly. Some children who are under-responsive may work very hard to feel stimuli. Miller refers to these children as "sensory seekers" (Miller, 2006, p. 13), who bump into walls, touch children while standing in line, lean on tables, or bite on the tips of pens. Other children may appear "shut down" or extremely quiet as if they are in their own worlds when their need for sensory input becomes extreme.

Areas to Observe Related to Under-Responsiveness (Hyposensitivity)
(Check the areas that apply to the child)

- ☐ Does the child seem to seek out input such as bumping into things intentionally?
- ☐ Does the child seem to seek input by touching things a lot?
- ☐ Does the child seem "out of it" or in his own world?
- ☐ Does the child seem tired a lot?

Interventions for Addressing Challenges with Under-Responsiveness (Hyposensitivity)

- Give the child input so as to heighten her responsiveness to stimuli.
- Give the child opportunities for sensory input throughout the day such as hard, crunchy foods, deep pressure, or heavy work (ask him to carry a stack of books, move some chairs, etc.).
- Redirect the child from inappropriate activities to more appropriate ones.

Areas to Observe Related to Under-Responsiveness (Hyposensitivity)
(Check the areas that apply to you)

- ☐ Do I like to bump into things intentionally (seek input)?
- ☐ Do I like to touch things a lot?
- ☐ Do I sometimes feel out of it and in my own world?
- ☐ Do I feel tired a lot?

Interventions for Addressing Challenges with Under-Responsiveness (Hyposensitivity)

- Ask an occupational therapist or adult to help you determine what "input" helps you the most and how to get that input. Input means information you give to your brain in order to increase your ability to respond "just right" to situations. This may include deep pressure on your shoulders, chewing something hard or crunchy, or doing something active such as jumping before a challenging situation. If you will be entering a difficult environment, give yourself that input (or ask someone to help you get it) ahead of time.

- Build in opportunities for sensory input throughout the day. This might include making sure you eat hard, crunchy foods; lifting, pushing, or pulling heavy things (e.g., carry a heavy backpack, ask if you can help stack chairs, take a walk or run, chew gum, swing on a swing – even if you are older; you may have an old swing set in your backyard).

Moving from Information and Knowledge to Real-Life Practice

Now that you have helped the child explore her sensory system, or explored y our own sensory system, you are ready to move on to applying this to situations in "real life" as well as begin to look at the relationship between the sensory system and the emotion system. The following chapters are designed for an adult to work on with a child or for an older child to work on independently, to the extent possible. The worksheets are intended to act as guides for exploring sensory issues and the feelings they may be causing – in a therapy office, in a school environment, or at home – and subsequently develop ways to address them.

Adults can sit with a child to introduce the workbook and then give her time and space to work on the sheets on her own, or the adult can stay with the child throughout to assist her in working through the activities. As mentioned earlier, the workbook is useful **in the moment** when a child is struggling in school, as exhibited by bumping into other children; **in retrospect** after a child hides under a table in the cafeteria as a reaction to overwhelming noises and smells; or **in preparation for an event** such as a field trip or a holiday gathering.

Sensory overload or negative sensory experiences can cause a child to feel strong emotions (both positive and negative). Therefore, if you use the worksheets to problem solve in the moment, you will need to help the child de-escalate first. To do so, you may use calming phrases such as, "You seem really upset, let's figure out how to help your body feel better together." It is usually also helpful to give the child some time in a quiet place to de-escalate before trying to look through the worksheets together. It may also help to have different tools available. "Tools" may include something crunchy to chew, something hard to squish (a stress ball), a straw to chew on, and gum.

For your convenience, the items from the Areas to Observe sections on the previous pages have been combined into two checklists, which are included in the Appendix. The first, Getting to Know the Child's Sensory Self, is one that you can review on your own before assisting a younger child with the workbook (roughly preschool age through 7 years old).[1] The second checklist, Getting to Know My Sensory Self, is meant to be used with an older child (roughly 7 through 11) before you go through the text together. It may also be used for a child (roughly 11 and up) to review independently before exploring the information and interventions on her own.

These checklists provide a concrete introduction to sensory systems and challenges. It might also be helpful at this point to look at Table 3.1 together with the child, as the pictures of the sensory gang may further clarify the concept of sensory systems.

---

[1]   As mentioned earlier, all ages listed are meant to be used as a guide only. Children develop at their own unique rates. Some are able to comprehend concepts, issues, and interventions early. Others may benefit from assistance for a longer period of time to maximize their comprehension of the concepts discussed throughout this text.

CHAPTER 4

LET'S TALK ABOUT BIG EMOTIONS AND FIGURE OUT WHAT CAUSES THEM

Chapters 2 and 3 provided an overview of sensory systems, sensory processing, and sensory integration. Now that you have a better understanding of the sensory world, we are going to look at the interaction between sensory input and emotions. This relationship is complex at best. Some emotions do not appear to be exclusively related to sensory input, or to be related at all. Other emotions are directly related to an experience in the sensory world.

For example, if you are trying to shop for holiday presents on December 10 and the mall is a sea of people, long lines, loud noises, lots of bumping and pushing, and general chaos, you might begin to feel stressed. In this situation, the input of all of the noise and commotion would probably trigger big emotions. These emotions might be exacerbated if the day-to-day management of sensory input is a challenge in and of itself. This chapter will explore the relationship between sensory input and emotions, clarify the concept of stimuli and triggers, and provide a brief introduction to the concept of the intensity of emotions. Later in this book, we will revisit emotional regulation in more depth.

Let's think for a moment about Sue (see pages 7-8). As she walked through the hallway, she experienced smells, textures, sounds, and bumps. In addition, there was a lot of visual information to process. If Sue's sensory system wasn't functioning *perfectly,* and she had trouble processing and integrating any of the information she received, her feelings may have looked like the chart on the next page.

Obviously, that is a lot of feelings to experience in a 2-½-minute period of time. Experiencing this many feelings may even pull Sue off task once she is in class, which can cause big feelings in addition to the ones she was already feeling just from walking through the hallway. It is important, then, to recognize these feelings so that a plan can be put in place to lessen them.

Let's take the feeling of nervousness for a moment. A plan for dealing with nervous feelings may include:

1. Identify the level of nervousness the person is feeling. (*intensity*)

2. Determine the situations that cause intense nervous feelings. (*stimuli and triggers*)

3. Select strategies that may be helpful in the particular situation. (*interventions*)

Let's take a closer look at the intensity of emotions.

Input	Sensory System	Feeling
Friend yelling "hi"	Auditory	Surprised, Happy
Bumped	Tactile, vestibular, proprioceptive	Annoyed
Flickering light	Visual, vestibular	Anxious
Looked at time	Visual, vestibular	Worried
Locker combination	Visual, tactile	Frustrated
Flying book	Visual, auditory	Scared
Slimy	Tactile	Sick
Slamming	Auditory	Startled
School dance sign	Visual	Nervous, excited
Lunch	Gustatory, olfactory	Disgusted

Note: Sensory gang used with permission. ©AAPC

Intensity

Identifying the level or intensity of a feeling is one of the most important steps toward developing strategies for dealing with feelings. Children are often blindsided by intense feelings and don't realize how big they are until after they've acted upon them. These actions are usually inappropriate or maladaptive in some way (such as aggression or yelling), and rather than decreasing the emotion, they actually tend to increase it (and get the child into trouble).

If a child understands that certain stimuli make his emotions feel bigger, he can face a situation better prepared, rather than feeling caught by surprise. Determining the intensity of a feeling can also help children understand the importance of intervening earlier (for example at a "1-2" on the following scale) before the feeling gets too big to handle.

Using a scale is often the clearest way to help a child recognize the existence and intensity of feelings. Scales are clear, visual, and provide a more universal way to talk about feelings. Several helpful scales are available. For example, Kari Dunn Buron and Mitzi Curtis (2004) have created a 5-point scale to assist children (and the adults who spend time with them) with identifying specific situations that create stress or anxiety so that they can then problem solve around these situations.

There are many ways to utilize Buron and Curtis's stress scale to explore feelings. The scale can be used in the moment, in retrospect, or in preparation for a potentially stressful event. Regardless of when and where it is used, it is helpful first to identify the stressful situation, determine at what level the child's emotions are, and then write the situation (or have the child write it) on the scale.

As you will see throughout this book, there are many opportunities to take down this information and determine what strategies might be helpful at each level or intensity of emotion. Regular use of this scale will help the child identify the intensity of her feelings in multiple environments such as home, school, social situations, and in the community.

As you work on the scale, please keep in mind that it can also be helpful for identifying situations that do not cause intense negative emotions but rather cause intense positive emotions. This is important because intense emotions can be associated with stress or difficulties regardless of whether the emotions are positive or negative. For example,

The Stress Scale

5 I could lose control

_____

4 Can really upset me

_____

3 Makes me nervous

_____

2 Bugs me

_____

1 Never bothers me

From: *The Incredible 5-Point Scale: Assisting Students with Autism Spectrum Disorders in Understanding Social Interactions and Controlling Their Emotional Responses* by K. D. Buron and M. Curtis, 2004, Shawnee Mission, KS: Autism Asperger Publishing Company. Used with permission.

the anticipation of a birthday party may cause happy or excited feelings, but if the intensity of these emotions is really high, the child may be unable to switch his thoughts from thinking about his birthday to concentrating in class. These difficulties in combination with the intense excitement may cause the child to feel a lot of stress.

It is also important to identify situations that keep a child at a "1" or a "2" as you work on the scale as they may help to ultimately mitigate stressful situations. For example, let's say that we have discovered that reading helps Max keep his body at a "1" or a "2." One day, Max's sister knocked over a block creation it had taken him an hour to build. If Max wrote this situation on the stress scale, he would write it next to the "5."

His mom, realizing how stressed, angry, and upset he was, recommended Max spend some time in his room reading. Her hope was that since reading typically kept his body calm, it would decrease the stress he was feeling as a result of his block creation getting ruined. The strategy worked! After reading, Max felt less stressed, and he was able to rebuild the building in his room so his sister couldn't get to it.

Stimuli and Triggers Can Cause Feelings – What Does This Really Mean?

Many of the worksheets in the rest of this book ask you to think about feelings a person may experience as a result of stimuli he has encountered.

 Facilitators: You may be thinking, "How am I going to explain *stimuli* to the child?"

 Explorers: You may be thinking, "What does *stimuli* really mean?"

Let's take a look at what the word *stimuli* means. First of all, *stimuli* is the plural *stimulus*; that is, it indicates that we are dealing with more than one. If you look up the word *stimulus* in Roget's New Millennium Thesaurus (http://thesaurus.reference.com/help/faq/roget.html), you may find such words as *bang, catalyst, kick, incitement, wave maker, impulse, spark plug*.

I find it helpful to think of a stimulus as a "wave maker." If you throw a large rock into the water, it creates a wave. The rock is the **stimulus** that **caused** the wave.

STIMULUS   RESULT

Similarly, a strong smell of perfume may cause you to feel sick:

STIMULUS   RESULT

But the smell of newly baked chocolate chip cookies may make you feel happy (and hungry):

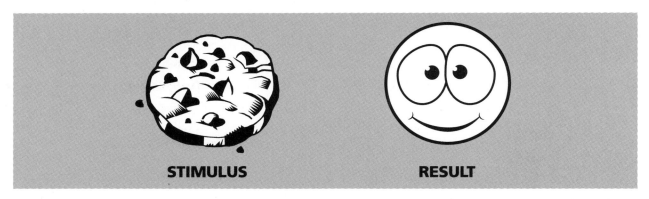

STIMULUS   RESULT

So, a stimulus is something that CAUSES you to feel a certain way, think a certain thing, or do a certain thing. And, *stimuli are more than one stimulus.* So . . . you may smell the chocolate chip cookies, feel happy and hungry, think, "that smells delicious," and run right into the kitchen to get one to eat. Yum!

Stimuli are also called TRIGGERS. A TRIGGER is also something that causes you to feel a certain way, think a certain thing, or do a certain thing.

Using the example above, we could say that the smell of the chocolate chip cookies *TRIGGERED* you to *FEEL* happy and hungry so you *ATE* one.

Facilitators: Many of the worksheets throughout this book will ask you to help the child explore a variety of stimuli or triggers and the feelings they might cause. The Feelings Chart in the Appendix (see page 141) can help with these activities. It may be useful to explore the different feelings by acting them out, thinking of situations that have caused feelings, or reading some of the books listed on pages 153-155 and discussing the different feelings encountered in the books. You can probably find many of these books at your local library. You can write (and draw) descriptions of feelings in the chart on page 52 to help clarify feelings and write what generally causes people to have those feelings. Take a moment to help the child identify triggers in her everyday life and the feelings they cause her. The triggers can be sensory related or be related to other daily events. You can do this using the Trigger Chart on page 53. You can then rate the feeling using the stress scale on page 47.

Explorers: As you can see, you will be asked to talk about feelings on some of the worksheets in the book since *STIMULI* and *TRIGGERS* can cause lots of different feelings. I know this may not be your favorite topic of conversation, but it is really helpful to figure out your feelings so you can decide what to do with them. Understanding your feelings and controlling them is not easy, but it is far better to **take control** of your feelings than to let your feelings control you.

If you are having trouble figuring out this mysterious world of feelings, you may want to ask an adult such as a parent, teacher, or member of your family to help you. I have listed some children's books on pages 153-155 that talk about things that trigger feelings and have great pictures of feeling faces. You may think, "Those are way too young for me" and you may be right. But they can help you make a little more sense of feelings. I bet your parents still have your old children's books somewhere in the house, or perhaps they can help you check some out of the library. You can also use the Feelings Chart in the Appendix (see page 141) as you work on the activities throughout this book.

Once you feel you understand the world of feelings, you can describe (and draw) feelings on the next page and write things that may cause people to have those feelings. Take a moment and write down triggers in your everyday life and identify the feelings they cause you to feel. The triggers can be sensory related or simply things that happen in your life. You can write this on the Trigger Chart on page 53. You can also rate the feelings using the Stress Scale on page 47.

A Quick Look at the Things That Trigger My Feelings

I think _____ means _____
               feeling   describe the feeling

_____. It seems people usually feel this way

when the following happens: _____
                                  name things that can trigger this feeling

_____.

Draw a picture of feeling

I think _____ means _____
               feeling   describe the feeling

_____. It seems people usually feel this way

when the following happens: _____
                                  name things that can trigger this feeling

_____.

Draw a picture of feeling

I think _____ means _____
               feeling   describe the feeling

_____. It seems people usually feel this way

when the following happens: _____
                                  name things that can trigger this feeling

_____.

Draw a picture of feeling

Trigger Chart

Trigger	Feelings (positive or negative)	Stress Rating (1-5)
My sister knocked over my blocks.	Angry, Furious, Upset	5

Facilitators and Explorers: This chapter provided an introduction to the idea that we all have many different feelings (positive and negative) that can impact us each day. We also looked at the fact that there are stimuli or triggers that can cause us to feel, think, or do certain things. Finally, we began to explore the INTENSITY of feelings.

In the next two chapters, we will explore how your body reacts to various stimuli, or triggers. After you become more familiar with whether you tend to over-react, under-react, or react "just right," you will get the chance to practice (or help the child practice) exploring feelings, feeling intensity, and feeling strategies further.

CHAPTER 5

THE ART OF SENSORY MODULATION –
OVER-REACTIVE, UNDER-REACTIVE, OR "JUST RIGHT"

Facilitators and Explorers: The following worksheets will help you develop a better understanding of your (and the child's) system of sensory modulation/regulation. Sometimes our bodies react more to things than they do at other times. As we mentioned earlier, this reaction can occur when our brains do not process information accurately, thus causing our brain (the traffic officer) to send inaccurate messages to our body, as shown in the example on page 4. Here is another example of the three scenarios that might occur when information is processed, all having to do with the tactile system (touch).

My Three Reactions

		OVER-REACT Wake up. Move quickly. "OUCH!"
SENSORY STIMULI (Nigel gently put his hand on Meetha's shoulder after he found out her dad died.)	**MEETHA'S CENTRAL NERVOUS SYSTEM**	**UNDER-REACT** Slow down. Getting very sleepy? "Did he touch my shoulder?"
		JUST RIGHT Be calm; Don't go too fast. Don't go too slowly. "That was nice of him."

Let's take a moment to explore each of these three reactions.

In the sensory world, fluctuations in our reactions are often related to both internal and external input. Internal input includes our circadian rhythm (our "body clock," which changes throughout the day and helps our body know when to calm itself for sleep or rouse itself for being awake), a full stomach, or the rush/receding of adrenaline. External input includes loud noises, pungent odors, lots of posters on the wall, or someone tapping a pencil. A child – or an adult for that matter – may either shut down and crawl into her "shell," or rev up and begin to bounce around, depending upon the message her brain sends to her body.

In 1996, Mary Sue Williams and Sherry Shellenberger introduced the concept of engine speeds to the world of occupational therapy. Engine speeds is part of their *Alert Program*®, a curriculum that assists people in regulating their bodies to function more effectively throughout the different aspects of their lives. Since the introduction of this concept more than 15 years ago, Williams and Shellenberger have continued to offer helpful information regarding self-regulation, sensory issues, and ways to incorporate the *Alert Program*® into home, school, and community environments. For more information about the *Alert Program*®, please refer to the following text: *How Does Your Engine Run?*® *A Leader's Guide to the Alert Program*® *for Self-Regulation* (Williams & Shellenberger, 1996). You may also visit the following website for more information: wwwAlertProgram.com.

I have found this concept of engine speeds helpful in my work with children who are attempting to understand their feelings, their bodies, self-regulation, and their sensory worlds. In this chapter, we will look further at self-regulation and whether our brain/body over-reacts, under-reacts, or reacts "just right" to triggers. Williams and Shellenberger (1996) discussed the concept of arousal, describing arousal as "a state of the nervous system, describing how alert one feels" (Williams & Shellenberger, 1996, pp. 1-5). For the sake of simplicity and clarity, I will be using the words *arousal, alert,* and *energy* interchangeably to describe the general way our body feels as it relates to our ability to concentrate, focus, and attend to tasks.

Over-React

Sometimes our central nervous system is "wired" in such a way that we tend to over-react to stimuli. This tendency to over-react may cause our arousal level or level of alertness (Williams & Shellenberger, 1996) to run too high. This higher level of energy or arousal might also occur in response to an emotional experience such as getting an A+ on a test. We might feel this higher level of alertness at different times of the day, depending upon the internal and external factors mentioned above.

Under-React

Sometimes you may feel completely exhausted or "out of it" – as if you are moving very slowly and have no energy. Unless it is nighttime and we are going to bed, it is at these times that we often need to do something to jump-start our bodies. We might get up and move around, suck on a piece of candy, or eat a meal or a snack. That usually jump-starts our bodies and brings our alertness back up to what we will call a "just right" level.

"Just Right"

Our "just right" level of arousal or alertness helps us respond to tasks and situations in an appropriate way. Our movements are neither too fast nor too slow; our energy is just right.

How Is My Body Reacting?

Facilitators: Please go through this worksheet with the child and assist him in filling it out. It may be helpful to act out what over-reacting, under-reacting, and reacting "just right" look like to help make the concept clearer. You can even give the child a drumstick or a pen and have him tap over-reacting, under-reacting, or re-acting "just right" by rapidly calling out one of the reaction types. This will give the child a clearer idea of what each of these reaction levels feels like.

Help the child choose which way his body feels most of the time and circle it. Then have him determine how he feels/what he does when he over-reacts, under-reacts, or reacts "just right."

Explorers: On pages 58-59, please circle the way your body feels most of the time. Then write how you feel/what you do when you over-react, under-react and react "just right." (You can look at the examples for ideas.)

Sometimes my brain tells my body to over-react, and my body goes too fast.
Zoom! Zoom! Zoom! Zoom! Zoom! Zoom!

**Sometimes my brain tells my body to under-react,
and my body goes too slowly.**

zzzzzzzzzzzzzzzzzzzzzzzzzzzzzzzzzzzzzzzzzzzzzzzzzzzzzzzzzzzzzzzzzzzzz

**Sometimes my brain tells my body to react evenly and calmly,
and my body feels "just right."**

aaahh aaahh aaahh aaahh aaahh aaahh

Zoom! Zoom! Zoom! Zoom! Zoom! Zoom!

When my body goes too fast, I usually:

(Here are some possible examples: Hit, yell, get into other people's space, cry, feel angry, have trouble thinking)

_____

_____

ZZZZZZZZZZZZZZZZZZZZZZZZZZZZZZZZZZZZZZZZZZZZZZZZZZZZZZZZZZZZZZZZZZZZZZZ

When my body goes too slowly, I usually:

(Here are some possible examples: Feel tired, hit, have trouble thinking, get frustrated easily)

_____

_____

aaahh aaahh aaahh aaahh aaahh aaahh

When my body feels "JUST RIGHT," I usually:

(Here are some possible examples: Stay calm, use words to ask for things, feel good, think clearly)

_____

_____

What Does My Body Look Like?

Facilitators: It can be helpful to draw things to help the child develop a deeper understanding of a concept. The following instructions are designed for an Explorer to read, but they will give Facilitators information about ways in which they can help the child they are working with complete the next activity and gain further insight into her sensory regulation/modulation.

Explorers: Sometimes it is helpful to draw things so that you can try to understand them better. You may think to yourself, "Hey, this is something I did when I was little." True, but drawing can help you look at things in a different way than just thinking about them. The following instructions will help you complete the next activity, which is designed to help you understand your ability to regulate/modulate the sensory information in your world.

What Does My Body Look Like?

Now that you have a better idea of how you typically react to stimuli, let's think about **what your body looks like** depending upon how you are reacting. In the blank space on page 62, draw a couple of pictures of your body. It can be a stick figure or a more detailed drawing of you. (You can use the pictures of bodies in the Appendix on pages 144-146 if you don't want to draw a picture yourself.)

You can use red to color in the parts of your body that are moving too fast (for example, your heart, your brain/thoughts), yellow to color the parts that are moving too slowly, and green to color in the parts that are moving "just right." You can choose other colors if you wish. You are also welcome to draw three separate pictures of your body. One that shows you moving "too fast," one that shows you moving "too slowly," and one that shows you moving "just right."

As you draw your picture(s), it may be helpful to think about the following questions:

- Is my body feeling fast, too slow, or "just right"?
- Am I having a hard time concentrating today or has it been easy to concentrate?
- Are things that don't normally bother me bothering me a lot right now?

(Draw below)

Reviewing My Body

Facilitators: This worksheet was designed for Explorers to use independently. However, if you feel the child with whom you are working is able to go through the questions with your assistance, feel free to use it.

Explorers: Now you will have the chance to think a bit more about your body and pinpoint ways your body's reaction interferes with your daily life and ways it enhances your life.

In general, do you tend to feel like you are bouncing around and full of energy, or do you tend to feel like it is a struggle to get through the day because your body feels slow and sluggish? Or do you feel "in between"? Please check your answer below.

I usually feel:

☐   **bouncy and energetic**

☐   **slow and sluggish**

☐   **"in between"**

Bouncy and Energetic

If you checked feeling bouncy and energetic throughout the day, think about whether there are times when this seems to interfere with what you need to do or whether it helps you get through the day. You can figure this out by thinking about whether or not an adult or friend asked you to settle down, calm down, sit still, do your work, listen, follow directions, or play by the rules. If people ask you to do these things a lot throughout the day, chances are the level of your reactions and energy is interfering with what you need to do.

Areas Where My Bounciness and High Energy May Be a Problem

Place a check mark next to the activities that your bounciness or high energy seem to interfere with or that are hard for you. There is space to add other areas where you think your high level of energy may be a problem for you:

☐ listening to the teacher in class

☐ talking with my friends

☐ getting my class work done

☐ getting my homework done

☐ completing the chores my mom or dad have asked me to do

☐ following directions

☐ _____

☐ _____

☐ _____

Areas Where My Bounciness and High Energy Are Helpful

There may also be times when your high level of energy seems to help you accomplish things. Please check off areas where your tendency to be bouncy and energetic assists you in your everyday activities. There is again space to add other areas you think are helped by your level of energy.

☐ sports

☐ staying up late to get something done

☐ getting through a lot of activities in one day

☐ getting from one place to another really quickly

☐ _____

☐ _____

☐ _____

How can you tell if other people are noticing your high level of energy?

Please check off the situations below that have happened to you and give an example in the space provided.

☐ People comment on my high level of energy by saying:

"_____

_____."

☐ I seem to get into trouble a lot.

For example: _____

_____

☐ I am asked to calm down a lot, particularly in certain situations, such as:

_____

_____

☐ Sometimes people around me (my parents, teacher, or friends) seem to look angry or frustrated with me. (You may want to describe the way they looked or the things they did that made you think they were feeling angry or frustrated.)

_____

_____

Slow and Sluggish

If you circled feeling slow and sluggish, think about ways this might impact your day. Place a check mark next to the activities with which it seems to interfere or that are hard for you. There is also space to add other areas where you think feeling slow and sluggish may be a problem for you.

Areas Where Being Slow and Sluggish May Be a Problem

☐ understanding what the teacher is saying in class

☐ talking with my friends

☐ getting my class work done on time

☐ getting my homework done on time

☐ completing the chores my mom or dad have asked me to do

☐ _____

☐ _____

☐ _____

Areas Where Being Slow and Sluggish Can Be Helpful

There may also be times when your low level of energy seems to help you accomplish things. Please check off the ways your tendency to be slow and sluggish assists you in your everyday activities. There is again space to add other areas you think are helped by your low level of energy.

☐ sitting quietly in class

☐ standing quietly in line

☐ sleeping well

☐ watching my favorite television show

☐ _____

☐ _____

☐ _____

How can you tell if other people are noticing your low level of energy?

Please check off the situations below that have happened to you and give an example in the space provided.

☐ People comment on my low level of energy by saying:

" _____

_____."

☐ I seem to get into trouble a lot.

For example: _____

_____

☐ I am asked to talk louder or talk more. This seems to happen in the following situations:

_____

_____

☐ Sometimes people around me (my parents, teachers or friends) seem to look frustrated with me. (You may want to describe the way they looked or the things they did that made you think they were frustrated.)

_____

_____

"In Between"

If you circled "in between," you may want to fill out both checklists to see how feeling slow and sluggish and feeling bouncy and energetic impact your daily life.

Once you have a better idea of how your body is doing, you can begin to think about the things that impact your body and what to do to speed your body up or slow your body down.

If you like drawing, you can draw a picture on the rest of this page of what you think your sensory body may look like. You can draw your body and then decide which of your senses (or Sensory Gang members) you think are generally over-reactive, under-reactive, or react "just right." A sample body is in the Appendix on page 143.

(Draw below)

Exploring the World Around Me

On the next worksheet, we will explore things that may affect your brain and body in both a positive and a negative way.

🖊 **Facilitators:** The next worksheet looks at specific stimuli that may impact the child such as plants, ceiling fans, or standing too close to someone. Please read the directions in the Explorer section for ways to use these pictures on other worksheets throughout the book.

🔍 **Explorers:** Hopefully, the pictures on page 71 will help you identify things that really bother you and things that you really like. (These pictures are also included in the Appendix on page 147.) You can laminate them and cut them out so you can move them around through the rest of the book. These pictures might help you to identify and think about items and situations that trigger you to feel a particular way, depending upon whether you over-react, under-react, or react "just right" to them.

Some of the items may cause your body to over-react or under-react, and others may not bother you at all. Some of the pictures may cause you to have an immediate negative feeling or an immediate positive one. You can move the pictures around throughout the rest of the workbook to identify what you hear, see, taste, feel, and smell in your environment as these items may be changing your level of energy or alertness. For example, when you hear the buzz of the lights in the classroom, your brain may tell your body to over-react and make it difficult for you to get your schoolwork done.

At the very least, the things we identify with our five senses may cause us to become distracted and have difficulty focusing. Therefore, it is worth exploring these items to identify if they are pulling you off track when working on a task. Feeling pulled off task can cause you to feel big feelings.

Exploring Things That Impact My Body and My Reactions

Facilitators: Look at the following pictures with the child. Discuss which of the items represented in the pictures cause the child to move faster or move more slowly. You can again remind the child that things that cause her to over-react probably increase her heart and breathing rate while things that cause her body to under-react may decrease her heart and breathing rate.

Explorers: Take a look at the pictures on page 71 and decide which of these things may cause your body to move faster or move more slowly. If you are having trouble deciding whether or not the things the pictures represent cause you to over- or under-react, try thinking about how fast your heart and breathing go when you think about the objects. Your heart and breathing will probably be faster when you over-react and slower if you under-react.

Note: If you cover up half of the page so that you can only see half of the pictures, it might help you think about the pictures more clearly.

cars/trucks/jeeps/traffic

rain

buzzing/bright lights

plants/inside/outside

water/getting wet

ceiling fans/other fans

motorcycles

music

standing in line/
others too close

fire alarm/other alarms

fruit/veggies/
foods I don't like

mushy/things I don't
like touching

crowds

bad smells

seeing my favorite toy

What Do You See? What's Your Reaction?

Explorers and **Facilitators:** Take a moment to look around the room you are in. In the chart below, write down some of the things you see or that the child sees. Then write down whether you/your child feels the items would trigger an over-reacting, under-reacting, or "just right" reaction.

Objects	Body

Understanding Your Reactions Leads to Sensory and Emotional Modulation/Regulation

Facilitators: Now that you and the child have listed the items in the room that impact the child's body and ability to react, you have hopefully built a foundation of new knowledge in the child that will assist you in completing the next series of worksheets.

Explorers: Now that you have listed the items that you noticed in the room and determined how they would impact your body and your ability to react "just right," you are hopefully developing an idea of how the things around you are affecting you. This knowledge will help you as you move through the next group of worksheets.

Note: Once you have a better idea of what things cause you to over-react and under-react, you can begin to explore whether those same things create large feelings (can be both positive and negative feelings). The more you understand about the things that impact you in both a helpful and a harmful way, the more you will be able to put strategies in place to counteract or to assist you with dealing with negative stimuli (things that impact you). This will help you keep your body feeling "just right" and help you manage your emotions better.

For example, if you determine that being around a large crowd of people is very stressful because the noise and the pushing overstimulate you and cause you to over-react to minor things, you might decide to arrive to an event early and leave again before everybody gets there. If this is not possible, you may experiment with chewing gum and putting weights in the pocket of your coat. The gum and the weights[1] might give your body the input you need to be able to be in a crowd without feeling overwhelmed and overstimulated. That is, it will help you with sensory and emotional modulation/regulation.

The key to sensory and emotional regulation is to (a) recognize the triggers, (b) know whether you tend to over- or under-react to the triggers, and (c) find strategies that help you manage the triggers so you can keep your feelings, level of alertness, and reactions "just right."

---

[1] Have an occupational therapist help determine the appropriate weight.

THE CONNECTION BETWEEN WHAT I HEAR, SEE, TASTE, FEEL, AND SMELL AND THE WAY MY BODY FEELS

A Journey Through the Five Senses

Facilitators: Pages 79-88 will give you the opportunity to more thoroughly explore the child's senses. You can assist the child in identifying smells, tastes, sounds, textures, or objects that he is noticing, by either looking through the environment in which you are working or thinking about a particular environment that has posed difficulties in the past. You can also think in general of things the child hears, sees, tastes, feels, and smells that may or may not bother him. You can then have the child write the words or draw a picture of these stimuli. You can also write or draw for the child. You might also use the pictures on page 71 or in the Appendix on page 147.

Once you (or the child) have written the words or drawn the pictures to represent things that the child detected through one or more of the five senses in the "stimuli" column, write the feeling or feelings it caused in the next column. This allows you to determine the things that are bothering the child and the things that are not. From there, you can explore the child's body by talking about different body parts and whether they are moving slowly, quickly, or "just right." Don't forget to talk about things you cannot see, such as the child's heartbeat, breathing rate, and his thoughts. At the bottom of each page of new stimuli, circle which way the child's body seems to be as a result of the things she heard, saw, felt, tasted, or smelled. Last, look through the strategies on the next page and determine which of them may be helpful. You can write these strategies in the "strategy" column. You can also add strategies to the strategy pages themselves.

Note: You can complete the following pages based on:

- something that is happening right now;

- something that happened in the past by thinking of past events as you and the child fill out the worksheets; or

- something that will be happening in the future by thinking of an event that may cause the child stress and coming up with strategies that might help the child in that moment.

Explorers: Pages 79-88 will take you on a journey through your five senses. You will be asked to draw pictures or write words to represent things that you hear, see, taste, feel, and smell. These can be things you are aware of and/or things that are bothering you. You can either pull these items out of the environment in which you are currently working or think of a place that has been particularly hard for you and try to remember what you heard, saw, tasted, felt, or smelled there. You can also think in general of things you hear, see, taste, feel, and smell that may or may not bother you.

Take a moment to write the words or draw pictures of the stimuli that you are noticing. You can also use the pictures on page 71 or in the Appendix on page 147 if you wish.

Once you have written the words or drawn the pictures of things that you detected through one or more of your five senses in the "stimuli" column, you can write the feeling or feelings they caused in the next column. That enables you to determine which stimuli are bothering you and which ones are not.

Remember, stimuli are things that CAUSE you to FEEL, THINK, or DO certain things. Stimuli cause "waves" of feelings, thoughts, and actions in your body.

You also have to decide how your body feels – whether your body is moving too slowly, too quickly, or "just right," depending upon what you hear, see, taste, feel, and smell. After you decide how your body is, circle it on the bottom of the page.

Hint: You can check whether your heart is beating very quickly or not, if your thoughts are racing or not, how your breathing is, or whether sitting still and concentrating has become challenging. This will help you to determine how your body is.

Review the strategies listed on the pages following each sense that might help your body feel "just right" and decide which strategies have helped you in the past or which strategies you think would help you now or in the future. Then write them into the "strategies" column. You can also add strategies to the bottom section of the strategy pages.

Note: You can complete the following pages based on:

- something that is happening right now by using what you wrote or drew on previous pages in the workbook to help you problem solve the current situation;

- something that happened in the past by thinking of past events as you fill out the worksheets;

- or something that will be happening in the future by thinking of an event that may cause you stress and coming up with a strategy that might help you.

Explorers and Facilitators:

Please Note: The pages discussing "eyes" or your visual sense are a bit different from the other pages. Often, the things you see are simply distractions rather than something upsetting. For example, if you are listening to the teacher and out of the corner of your eye you see a bird land on the windowsill, it may not cause you to feel a particular way, or even change how you react, but it may still distract you from what the teacher was saying. This distraction may last seconds or minutes. If the distraction was quite short (seconds), and it was something relatively neutral such as a bird, it may not have caused you to feel anything in particular. However, if the distraction was longer and caused you to miss important information, it may have caused you to feel stressed or anxious about the missed material.

It is hard to know what will be simply distracting and what may cause you (or the child) to feel strong emotions, so it is important to figure out all of the things in your (or the child's) environment that may be distracting. In general, your visual sense (or the child's) is probably one of your (or the child's) strengths!

What I Can Hear with My Ears

Stimuli	Feelings		Strategies
	Positive Feelings	Negative Feelings	

When I hear something that bothers me, my body goes: (circle one)

Fast

Slow

"Just right"

Strategies for Dealing with Sounds That Bother Me

If I hear something that bothers me, I can:

- Ask, "What is that noise?"

- Take a break in a quiet place.

- Ask to listen to a book on tape.

- Ask if the noise can be turned off.

- Wear ear plugs (soft foamy ones).

- Listen to music.

Other Strategies That Help
(Write your own/child's ideas here)

What I See with My Eyes

Stimuli	Feelings		Strategies
	Positive Feelings	Negative Feelings	

When I see something that bothers me, my body goes: (circle one)

Fast

Slow

"Just right"

Strategies for Dealing with Visual Things That Bother Me

If I see something that distracts me and causes me to feel upset, I can:

- Ask, "What is that?"

- Take a break in a quiet place.

- Move my desk closer to the front of the room.

- Take some deep breaths.

Other Strategies That Help
(Write your own/child's ideas here)

What I Can Taste with My Tongue and My Mouth

Stimuli	Feelings		Strategies
	Positive Feelings	Negative Feelings	

When I taste something that bothers me, my body goes: (circle one)

Fast

Slow

"Just right"

Strategies for Dealing with Tastes That Bother Me

If I taste something that bothers me, I can:

- Ask, "What is that?"

- Ask for a drink of water.

- Tell myself the taste will go away fast.

- Take some deep breaths.

Other Strategies That Help
(Write your own/child's ideas here)

What I Can Feel with My Finger or Other Parts of My Body
(such as your shoulders, your feet, your arm, etc.)

Stimuli	Feelings		Strategies
	Positive Feelings	Negative Feelings	

When I feel something that bothers me, my body goes: (circle one)

Fast

Slow

"Just right"

Strategies for Dealing with Touch and Textures That Bother Me

If I feel something that bothers me, I can:

- Ask, "What is that?"

- Count to 10 to calm down.

- Tell myself I don't need to be upset.

- Take some deep breaths.

Other Strategies That Help
(Write your own/child's ideas here)

What I Can Smell with My Nose

Stimuli	Feelings		Strategies
	Positive Feelings	Negative Feelings	

When I smell something that bothers me, my body goes: (circle one)

Fast   **Slow**   **"Just right"**

Strategies for Dealing with Smells That Bother Me

If I smell something that bothers me, I can:

- Ask, "What is that?"

- Find something that smells good to me like a piece of gum.

- Tell myself I don't need to feel irritated or anxious because the smell will be gone soon.

- Find something that might distract me, like sucking on a mint.

Other Strategies That Help
(Write your own/child's ideas here)

My Five Senses, Sensory Modulation, My Feelings, and Me

✏️ **Facilitators:** You can use the chart, Putting It All Together to Increase Sensory Modulation, on page 91 to summarize the discoveries you have made up until now with the child you are assisting. Add to the chart on an ongoing basis as situations arise that include stimuli that trigger feelings and impact the child's body and ability to regulate sensory input. You can write "over-react," "under-react," or "just right" in the Body Reaction column for each stimulus. For example, let's say the child went to a friend's house for a play date and had a really difficult time, including screaming at the other child. In discussing the situation, you find out that the friend's older sister was practicing the flute during the play date and determine that the noise of the flute was too difficult for the child to handle. Talking through the situation can assist you and the child in determining a strategy that might help the child at future play dates.

Note: Please don't forget to include stimuli that make or made the child happy or calm. It is helpful to know what makes one feel good, as positive stimuli may become strategies for dealing with difficult stimuli and difficult feelings.

For example, Penelope was leaving the playground after recess to go inside when a small black, oval rock caught her eye. She bent down and picked it up. It felt incredibly cool and smooth in her hands. She decided to put it in her pocket. Later that day, Fred began to tease Penelope as they walked into class. Penelope couldn't believe Fred was bothering her again, and she began to feel upset. Penelope happened to put her hand in her pocket and ran her fingers over the cool, smooth rock. She immediately began to feel calmer and decided that she wasn't going to let Fred's teasing bother her. She sat down at her desk, rock in hand, ready to hear what they were going to do in class that day. In this situation, the rock was a positive stimulus that counteracted Fred's negative teasing and Penelope's subsequent negative feelings.

Explorers: Now that you have explored your five senses – what you hear, see, taste, feel, and smell – you can fill in the chart, Putting It All Together to Increase Sensory Modulation, on page 91. This chart summarizes some of the discoveries you have made up till now in this workbook. Add to the chart on an ongoing basis to track the things that you are exposed to through your five senses, how they impact your body and your ability to regulate sensory input, and how they make you feel. You can write "over-react," "under-react," or "just right" in the Body Reaction" column for each trigger.

Remember, a stimulus is something that causes you to think, feel, or act in a different way. Throwing rocks (stimulus) into water causes a wave (action). Getting a new iPod (stimulus) causes you to feel excited (feeling).

For example, let's say you are at a football game as a spectator. You notice that the smell of the food around you is bothering you and causing you to feel irritable. The food is the stimulus that *causes* you to feel irritable. You may decide to write this on your chart when you come home so that you can choose a strategy for dealing with it the next time you attend a game.

Note: Please don't forget to include stimuli that make or made you happy or calm. It is helpful to know what makes you feel good, as positive stimuli may become strategies for dealing with difficult stimuli and difficult feelings.

For example, Penelope was leaving the playground after recess to go inside when a small black, oval rock caught her eye. She bent down and picked it up. It felt incredibly cool and smooth in her hands. She decided to put it in her pocket. Later that day, Fred began to tease Penelope as they walked into class. Penelope couldn't believe Fred was bothering her again, and she began to feel upset. Penelope happened to put her hand in her pocket and ran her fingers over the cool, smooth rock. She immediately began to feel calmer and decided that she wasn't going to let Fred's teasing bother her. She sat down at her desk, rock in hand, ready to hear what they were going to do in class that day. So, the rock helped her feel better. The rock was a POSITIVE stimulus.

Putting It All Together to Increase Effective Sensory Modulation

Stimulus/Trigger	Sense	Feeling	Body Reaction	Strategy/Tool
Food	Nose	Irritated	Over-react	Bring candy to suck on so the smell won't be as strong.
Flute	Ears	Upset	Over-react	Ask a grown-up for help (next time, maybe the older sister can practice the flute after you leave).

The more you understand the triggers that cause your body to over-react, under-react, or react "just right," the better you are able to pick helpful strategies. And the more you use these strategies or tools, the better you are able to regulate your sensory self.

CHAPTER 7

CONTROLLING MY BODY AND STAYING IN MY OWN SPACE

The next two sections explore the vestibular system (the system that helps us keep our body in control and in our own space) and the proprioceptive system (the system that helps our joints, muscles, and bodies work well). The worksheets look at how these systems impact the activities we do and the feelings we have – whether we over-react, under-react, or react "just right."

Vestibular System – The Balancing Act of Body Control

✏️ **Facilitators and** 🔍 **Explorers:** As described on page 32, our vestibular system gives us the information we need to know where we are relative to other people and objects in space as well as information about distance, movement, and location. It is the system that assists us with balance and the ability to coordinate movements between the left and right sides of our bodies.

For example, the soccer player on the right is standing and balancing on his left leg while kicking with his right. His arms are up to balance him, and he is turning his head toward the ball. His foot has to avoid the grass and hit the ball in order to kick it. If his vestibular system is working well, he will be able to kick the ball in the direction he wants it to go without falling down. If it is not working well, he may end up losing his balance and fall to the ground.

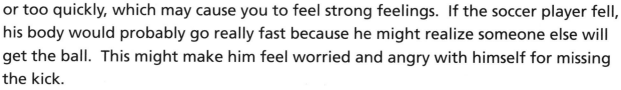

If your vestibular system is not functioning well, it may cause your body to operate either too slowly or too quickly, which may cause you to feel strong feelings. If the soccer player fell, his body would probably go really fast because he might realize someone else will get the ball. This might make him feel worried and angry with himself for missing the kick.

If you have issues with your vestibular system, entering the gym for P.E. probably makes you feel stressed. The majority of the activities in P.E. require any of the following movements: balancing, standing on one foot while kicking a ball, running and kicking at the same time, standing and swinging at the same time, and avoiding others as you run in a small space. In order to be able to complete any of these activities, your vestibular system needs to be operating accurately. If it is not, your body may either slow down too much or speed up too much, which may lead to big feelings.

Explorers: (**Facilitators:** The next series of questions may be helpful to review with your child.)

When you went through the checklists on pages 32-33 for controlling your body (vestibular system), did you think you have some difficulties in this area? (Please circle the appropriate answer.)

Yes   **No**   **Unsure** (I might need to ask someone to help me figure it out.)

If you said Yes or Unsure, please list some of the areas that are hard for you that you think might be related to this area.

_____

_____

_____

How do you react when you are in a situation that you listed as being hard for you? (For example, do you yell, ask to go to the bathroom, get a drink of water, avoid doing it?)

_____

_____

_____

How do you feel when you end up in a situation that is hard for you? (happy, sad, angry, overwhelmed, embarrassed, anxious, tired) You may even feel a combination of feelings. For example, if the soccer player fell, he might have felt angry with himself, upset that his teammates might be unhappy with him, worried that someone else will take the ball, and embarrassed over falling – all at the same time.

_____

_____

_____

What do you do to help yourself feel better if you are feeling a negative feeling? (take a break, ask for help, talk to a friend, talk to an adult?)

_____

_____

_____

Proprioceptive System – "Joints, Muscles, Body . . . Stand Up, Stay in Your Own Space, and Listen Up!"

✎ **Facilitators** and 🔍 **Explorers:** The proprioceptive system (see pages 33-34) helps us be aware of the sensations in our body parts so that we can use them effectively and most efficiently. It is the system that helps us keep our balance as a result of the information our joints and muscles send to our brains. It allows us to do things in a more automatic way rather than having to think about it or watch ourselves in order to accomplish it.

For example, if you have issues with your proprioceptive system, you might have trouble with dressing. If you think about how we take our pants off, we often stand up and either pull them off one leg at a time, sit down and lean over to pull them off, or stand up and use our feet to pull the opposite leg off. If you have trouble with your proprioceptive system, this seemingly simple, automatic task might seem complicated and require a lot of effort.

🔍 **Explorers:** (✎ **Facilitators:** The next series of questions may be helpful to review with your child.)

🔍 When you went through the checklists on page 34 for keeping your body in your own space (proprioceptive difficulties), did you think you have some difficulties in this area? (Please circle the appropriate answer.)

Yes **No** **Unsure** (I might need to ask someone to help me figure it out.)

If you said Yes or Unsure, please list some of the areas that are hard for you that you think might be related to your ability to use your muscles and joints (proprioceptive system).

_____

_____

_____

How do you react when you are in a situation that you listed as being hard for you? (For example, do you yell, ask to go to the bathroom, get a drink of water, avoid doing it, etc.)

_____

_____

_____

How do you feel when you end up in a situation that is hard for you? (happy, sad, angry, overwhelmed, embarrassed, anxious, tired) You may even feel a combination of feelings. For example, Jack asks you to the school dance. You are very excited because you really wanted him to ask you to go. On the night of the event, you get up to dance for the first slow song and can't seem to stop stepping on Jack's feet. You feel embarrassed, frustrated, and upset all at the same time.

_____

_____

_____

What do you do to help yourself feel better if you are feeling a negative feeling? (take a break, ask for help, talk to a friend, talk to an adult, etc.)

_____

_____

_____

FROM SENSORY MODULATION TO EMOTIONAL REGULATION –

A CLOSER LOOK AT TRIGGERS, INTENSITY OF FEELINGS, AND STRATEGIES FOR MAKING MY FEELINGS MORE MANAGEABLE

As discussed earlier, the distinction between sensory regulation/modulation and emotional regulation/modulation can be tricky at times. Many people ask me to help them distinguish whether or not a child has an underlying emotional issue or an underlying sensory issue. The purpose of this chapter is to assist you in helping the child find strategies that address the intensity of her emotions regardless of whether or not the trigger is sensory related. At the end of the chapter, we will briefly look at ways to sort out the differences between emotional and sensory regulation.

Please keep in mind that you can always use sensory interventions that might reduce reactivity and emotions such as squeezing putty, asking for deep pressure (massage) from an appropriate adult, doing jumping jacks or push-ups or going for a walk (as discussed throughout the book). The interventions in this chapter simply isolate the emotions (whether the trigger is a sensory trigger or not) in order to increase interventions that specifically address intensity. It is my belief that the combination of sensory strategies that potentially address an underlying issue combined with emotional strategies that address intensity is typically most effective.

Lowering the Intensity of Your Feelings in Order to Regulate Them

Facilitators: As we have seen throughout this book, the sensory reactions with which the child is struggling can cause big, powerful feelings. You have discussed the words *trigger* and *stimuli* with the child and hopefully given her a better understanding of what both of these words mean. You have also gone through specific examples of stimuli and triggers and the feelings they may cause.

At this point, you may want to remind the child of the relationship between triggers and feelings by talking about the examples of the chocolate chip cookies and the football game. You can use the pictures below to explain it more clearly. (Please keep in mind that the child will probably understand the picture stories better if you cover everything on the page except for the story you are reading. This will assist her with visual processing.)

The smell of the chocolate chip cookies TRIGGERED you to

FEEL happy and hungry , so you ATE one.

The smell of the food at the football game TRIGGERED you

to FEEL irritated . You decided to suck on a piece of candy

to help yourself feel better.

It is better to be in control of your feelings than to let your feelings be in control of you!

The next set of worksheets look at feelings and triggers. They are designed to have the child explore strategies that might help her feel better, and to assist you and the child in exploring the intensity (amount/strength) of her feelings. As mentioned in Chapter 4, recognizing the intensity of feelings is critical as strategies may change depending upon the intensity of our feelings. It is also important to explore intensity as our ability to make good decisions typically decreases as the intensity of our feelings increases. Conversely, as the strength of our feelings decreases, our ability to make good decisions increases. I often draw a bar graph such as the one below to explain this.

The Intensity of Your Feelings Affects Your Decision-Making Skills

If the intensity of your feelings is really high, your ability to make a good decision goes down.

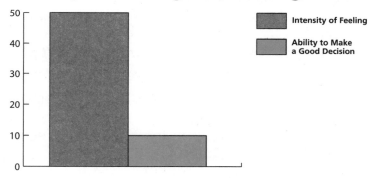

High Intensity = Bad Decision

If the intensity of your feelings is low, your ability to make a good decision goes up.

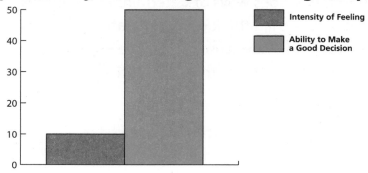

Low Intensity = Good Decision

You might also tell the child a story such as the one below to help him understand the concept of intensity better.

Imagine you just found out that your sister scratched your favorite DVD. You are so furious you could punch her – you could scream – you feel like you might lose control.

Right now, your ability to make a decision about what to do to your sister is not good. You are way too angry – the intensity of your anger is too big. It would probably be best to spend some time alone in your room until the intensity of your anger decreases. Maybe you need to hide under your covers, read a book, or draw a picture to calm down a bit. You might need help from an adult. Other strategies like taking a deep breath or counting to 10 may or may not work when your anger is that BIG.

Once your anger gets smaller, you will probably be able to deal with your sister and the scratched DVD in a positive way – a way that solves the problem instead of making it worse. If you punched her, that would definitely make it worse because she would be really upset and your mom would be, too.

Phew, you waited until you were a bit less angry and didn't punch your sister. You talked with her about how angry you were, and she decided to buy you a new DVD. Your mom said she would help, too. That worked out great!

We will be looking at three ways to examine the intensity of feelings – a Little-to-Big Pyramid (page 107), a Feelings Thermometer (page 108), and a Feelings Chart (pages 110-111). Review these three ways of measuring intensity to see which is the easiest to understand. You can also look back at the 5-point scale on page 47.

Before we proceed to the various ways of determining the intensity or strength of the child's feelings, help the child think of four situations/triggers and the feelings (positive or negative feelings) they caused. As in the example above, these triggers can be sensory in nature or not. Write them in the first two columns of the chart on page 106 under the example.

Explorers: As we have seen throughout this book, the sensory reactions with which we are struggling can cause us to feel really big, powerful feelings. As we discussed earlier, something that causes you to feel a certain way is called a "trigger." If we go back to the example of being at a football game and finding the smell of the food to be unpleasant, we say that the food was the *trigger* that caused *feelings* of irritation. You may also remember the example of the chocolate chip cookies. The smell of the cookies was the trigger that caused you to feel happy and hungry, and to eat some.

On the chart on page 91, Putting It All Together to Increase Sensory Modulation, you explored the stimuli or triggers that were impacting your feelings as well as your ability to respond with a "just right" reaction. You also saw how important it is to explore triggers and the feelings they can cause so that you can put a strategy in place to help make your feelings more manageable.

The next worksheets look at some of those feelings and triggers. They are designed to help you explore strategies that might help you feel better, and to assist you in exploring the intensity (amount/strength) of your feelings. It is helpful to explore the intensity of your feelings as your strategy may change depending upon the intensity of the feeling. It is also important to explore the intensity of your emotions as our ability to make good decisions typically decreases as the intensity of our feelings increases. Conversely, as the strength of our feelings decreases, our ability to make good decisions increases.

The Intensity of Your Feelings Affects Your Decision-Making Skills

If the intensity of your feelings is really high, your ability to make a good decision goes down.

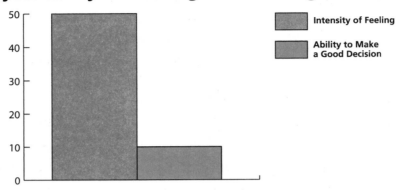

High Intensity = Bad Decision

If the intensity of your feelings is low, your ability to make a good decision goes up.

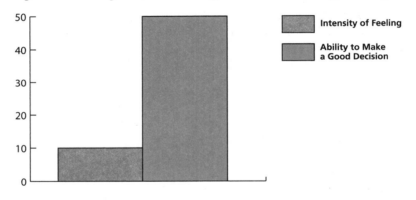

Low Intensity = Good Decision

Think of the following example:

You just found out that your sister scratched your favorite DVD. You are so furious you could punch her.

Right now, your ability to make a decision about the best way to handle this situation is not very good. You are too angry – the intensity of your anger is too big. It would probably be best to spend some time alone in your room until the intensity of your anger decreases. Other strategies like taking a deep breath or counting to 10 may or may not work when your anger is that BIG. Once your anger decreases, you will probably be able to deal with your sister and the scratched DVD in a way that better solves the problem.

Phew, you waited until you were a bit less angry and didn't punch your sister. You talked with her about how angry you were, and she decided to buy you a new DVD. That worked out great.

We will be discussing three ways to examine the intensity of feelings for you to experiment with – a Little-to-Big Pyramid, a Feelings Thermometer, and a Feelings Chart. You can decide which way of measuring the intensity of your feelings is most helpful for you. You may find that you like one of the ways one day and a different one another day.

Before we proceed to the different ways of determining the intensity or strength of your feelings, think of four situations/triggers (sensory or other, such as the example with the DVD above) and the feelings (positive or negative feelings) they caused. Write them in the first two columns in the following chart under the example.

Exploring How Intense My Feelings Can Get

Ways to Measure Intensity

Situation/ Trigger	Feeling(s)	Pyramid	Feelings Thermometer	Feelings Chart	Strategy
Example: Smell of food	• Irritated • Sick	• Medium • Little	• 4 • 2	• Medium • Low	• Suck on candy • Walk away for a moment
1.					
2.					
3.					
4.					

Ways to Measure Intensity

✏️ **Facilitators** and 🔍 **Explorers:** Keep the four situations/triggers and the feelings they caused in mind as you read through the following ways of identifying the intensity of your feelings. In the following Little-to-Big Pyramid (Jaffe & Gardner, 2006), we look at intensity through the use of three words: *little*, *medium*, and *big* placed on a pyramid. This framework helps determine the "size" of the feelings a person is feeling as it is visual and easy to understand.

Little-to-Big Pyramid

From: *My Book Full of Feelings* by A. Jaffe and L. Gardner, 2006, Shawnee Mission, KS: Autism Asperger Publishing Company. Used with permission.

✏️ **Facilitators:** Using the Little-to-Big Pyramid to figure out the intensity of feelings related to each trigger, go back to the chart on page 106 and write in the column labeled "pyramid," or help the child write, whether the feelings she experienced in the situations/triggers were "little," "medium," or "big." If the child discussed more than one feeling associated with the situations/triggers, please rate the intensity of each.

Explorers: Using the Little-to-Big Pyramid to figure out the intensity of your feelings related to each situation/trigger you listed, go back to the chart on page 106 and write in the column labeled "pyramid" whether the feeling or feelings you experienced in the situations/triggers were "little," "medium," or "big." If you wrote more than one feeling for the situations/triggers, rate the intensity of each.

Facilitators and Explorers: Another way to measure the intensity of feelings is to create a thermometer using a piece of masking tape. Place a long piece of tape across the floor and write the numbers 0 through 5 on it. If you are in a small space and need a smaller thermometer, draw a thermometer on a sheet of paper and use a paper clip or other small object to move up and down on the thermometer.

Feelings Thermometer

0	1	2	3	4	5

The first way to explore intensity is to pick an emotion and "act" out the different ways that emotion might look depending upon the intensity. For example, if I was acting out happy, my walk on the thermometer may look as follows:

0	1	2	3	4	5
No emotion	Small smile	Bigger smile	Big smile with loud, happy sigh	Big smile with happy shaking	Huge smile, jumping up and down

Facilitators: You can either act this out with the child or talk it through and write it out. It is much more effective to act it out if the child is willing to do so. You and the child can pick three feelings from the situations you wrote down and write or act out what the feeling might look like at each level of intensity. After you do that, go back to the chart on page 106 and write down, or have the child write down, the level of intensity that goes with each feeling the child experienced as a result of the situations/triggers. You can write these numbers in the column labeled Feelings Thermometer.

Explorers: I know it might be a little strange to act this out by yourself, so for this activity I suggest you ask an adult to help you. It is actually fun to act it out, but if you are uncomfortable, even with an adult helping you, you can think about it and perhaps even write it down on the thermometer in the Appendix on page 142. You can pick three feelings from the situations you wrote down, and write or act out what the feeling might look like at each level of intensity. After you do that, go back to the chart on page 106 and write down the level of intensity that goes with each feeling you experienced as a result of the situations/triggers. You can write these numbers in the column labeled Feelings Thermometer.

Facilitators and Explorers: The last method for helping you determine the intensity of your feelings uses pictures of emotions with the choice of a high, medium, or low amount of that emotion (see pages 110-111). It looks at the situation that caused the feeling and the intensity of the feeling.

Feelings Chart

HIGH, MEDIUM, LOW:
LOOK AT HOW HIGH THOSE FEELINGS CAN GO!

FEELING	INTENSITY	SITUATIONS
Angry	HIGH	
	MEDIUM	
	LOW	
Sad	HIGH	
	MEDIUM	
	LOW	
Nervous	HIGH	
	MEDIUM	
	LOW	

FEELING	INTENSITY	SITUATIONS
Scared	HIGH	
	MEDIUM	
	LOW	
Happy	HIGH	
	MEDIUM	
	LOW	
Calm	HIGH	
	MEDIUM	
	LOW	

Note: The concept of using shading to illustrate the intensity of feelings in this model is adapted from Jaffe and Gardner, *My Book Full of Feelings: How to Control and React to the Size of Your Emotions* (2006).

Facilitators: Look at the chart on pages 110-111 and help the child decide what emotion goes with the situations you discussed. Next, talk about how intensely the child might feel that emotion. After you decide together whether the child would experience the emotion as "high," "medium," or "low," write this on the chart in the column entitled Feelings Chart on page 106.

Now that you and the child have experimented with different ways to identify the intensity of his emotions, you can decide together if there was one method that worked the best. You may find that all of the strategies were helpful and can, therefore, alternate between them to decide on the intensity of the child's feelings. Have the child close his eyes and picture the Little-to-Big Pyramid, the Feelings Thermometer, and the Feelings Chart in his mind. Keep in mind that the most important thing for the child to take away from these strategies is a visual image. The visual image has the potential to help the child in different types of situations.

The more the image sticks in the child's mind, the more readily the child will be able to picture it in difficult moments.

Explorers: Think back to the four situations you thought of for these feeling intensity activities. Next, think about the emotions each situation might cause and decide what the intensity of those feelings was: "high," "medium," or "low." You can use the chart on pages 110-111 to help you decide. You can write "high," "medium," or "low" in the chart on page 106 in the column entitled Feelings Chart.

Now that you have experimented with different ways to identify the intensity of your emotions, decide whether there was one that you liked the best. You may find that you like all of the strategies and may alternate between using them to determine the intensity of your feelings. Close your eyes and take a moment to picture the Little-to-Big Pyramid, the Feelings Thermometer, and the Feelings Chart in your mind.

The most important thing to take away from these strategies is that you can create a visual image in your mind to carry with you from situation to situation. The more the image sticks in your mind, the more successful you will be at using it in the "heat of the moment."

Strategies That Match the Intensity of My Emotions

Facilitators: Throughout the book, you have worked with the child on various strategies and tried to decide which ones may help him in specific situations in which he is experiencing some sort of sensory stimuli or triggers. Now that the child has a better understanding of the intensity of his feelings, hopefully, it will be easier to decide together what strategies are most helpful in different situations. It is important to explain that triggers can "piggyback" on each other and increase the intensity of feelings rather quickly. The Appendix includes an activity that you can use to explain the "piggyback" effect of stimuli, called "My Cup Runneth Over" (see page 148).

It may also be helpful to go back to the chart on page 106 with the child and write in strategies for the feeling(s) you or the child listed. Help the child think of strategies that would help to decrease both her intense feelings and her less intense feelings. Some sample strategies for anger are listed below the pyramid format on page 114.

Explorers: Throughout the book, you have read through strategies and have thought about strategies of your own that may help you cope with the sensory input you are receiving and the sensory difficulties you are having. Now that you have a better understanding of the intensity of feelings, it is easier to decide which strategies are most helpful in different situations.

Triggers can "piggyback" on each other and increase the intensity of your feelings quite quickly. For example, let's say that the smell of the food during the game created a level "3" feeling of irritability. Then, as you were leaving the stadium, someone bumped into you. Since you were already at a "3," the intensity of your feelings immediately shot to a "5."

Since the intensity of feelings can increase quite rapidly, it is important to pick a strategy when the intensity of your feelings is still pretty low. The Appendix contains an activity that may help you better understand this "piggyback" effect, called "My Cup Runneth Over" (see page 148).

It may also be helpful to go back to the chart on page 106 and write in strategies for the feeling(s) you listed. Try to think of a strategy that would be helpful to decrease your intense feelings as well as your less intense feelings. Some sample strategies for anger are listed in the pyramid format below.

Anger

- Walk away
- Ignore it

- Play a game with myself by silently going through the alphabet, " a is for apple, b is for boat . . ."
- Distract myself by reading

- Ask for help
- Take deep breaths
- Chew gum
- Take a break

Remember, the strategy you put into place will help reduce the intensity (size) of your feelings, which will help your body and your reaction be "just right."

The better your feelings and your body feel, the better you will feel.

A Closer Look at Distinguishing Emotional Issues from Sensory Issues

The ability to determine whether a given behavior suggests an underlying emotional issue, such as being over-reactive or under-reactive emotionally, or an underlying sensory issue, is in many ways beyond the scope of this book. We will, however, take a brief look at this distinction.

If the child falls more into the realm of emotional regulation challenges, you may want to choose different interventions (or at least a different order of interventions) than if the child falls more into a sensory regulation realm. Let's first look at how a child's reaction to situations may change depending upon whether sensory or emotions are the underlying issue:

DIFFICULTY REGULATING EMOTIONS – Elyse

EMOTIONAL RESPONSE ⟶ SENSORY SENSITIVITY

Wanted a package to be on the front step, but there wasn't a package.

Mom tries to hug Elyse. Elyse screams "Don't touch me," and hits mom.

(SAD, DISAPPOINTED, ANGRY) ⟶ (TACTILE DEFENSIVENESS)

DIFFICULTY REGULATING SENSORY SYSTEM - Max

SENSORY SENSITIVITY ⟶ EMOTIONAL RESPONSE

Got home from school where the kids had been sitting very close to each other in a loud assembly for an hour. People had accidentally brushed their bodies against Max throughout the assembly.

Max went back to class, and a child dropped a book next to him by a mistake. Max started screaming and crying.

(AUDITORY AND TACTILE OVER-STIMULATION) ⟶ (ANGER, SADNESS)

In these examples, the interventions would look very different for Elyse than for Max. Specifically, the intervention for Elyse would focus on prevention and intervention. For example, the prevention might be to warn her that there might not be a package today and pre-plan a strategy that might help her deal with her emotions. The intervention might be: help her recognize the feeling she was feeling; offer a brief, clear strategy such as, "It looks like you are sad, disappointed, and angry; would you like a hug?"

The intervention for Max might also include prevention and intervention, but such efforts would be in the sensory realm rather than the emotional. The prevention might be offering headphones or earplugs and giving Max the option to sit in a place where there would be more space between him and the other children. The intervention might be to have Max carry books back to class (so-called "heavy lifting") after the assembly to give his body some input.

It is helpful to look for clues to determine whether emotional regulation or sensory regulation underlies the child's difficulties. The following vignette offers us the opportunity to look for such clues.

Josephine is a 2-½-year-old with speech/language delays. She had been receiving therapy from a speech/language pathologist (SLP) for three months, and both the SLP and Josephine's parents felt she wasn't making as much progress as expected after three months. Their concern centered on her "energy," fearlessness, and irritability. Josephine spent most of her day climbing up the furniture and jumping off again. She didn't seem to have any fear at all. Her parents worried she was heading toward a diagnosis that might ultimately require her to be on medication to help her calm down. They were even more concerned that she would hurt herself. She also presented as irritable a lot of the day and began to tantrum if her parents tried to redirect her from jumping.

Now that you have read the above scenario, you may want to take a moment to fill in the chart on the following page.

Emotional Regulation Signs	Sensory Regulation Signs

When I observed Josephine, I began to wonder whether her high activity level and repetitive jumping from high places were her attempts to give herself input. I decided to test out this hypothesis before pursuing the warning signs that perhaps an emotional issue was involved. As it turned out, the family had just received a package that had lots of packing popcorn in it. I asked if it was okay to let Josephine sit in the packing popcorn (and asked if she had a tendency to put things in her mouth; she didn't). Her parents said it was fine, and we let Josephine get into the box (it was rather large). She loved it. She jumped in the box, played with, squished, laid down in, and generally rolled all over the popcorn.

In the meantime, the SLP and I talked with Josephine to see if she'd imitate what we were saying. Amazingly, she began to imitate quite a bit. She also made a few requests to her mom for juice and food. It was wonderful. It was the most organized Josephine had been in a long time. So, we recommended an occupational therapy consult and I stepped back out of the interventions.

This case scenario is a dramatic example of the difference sensory input can make for a child. The input changed the way her parents viewed her entirely. Of course, it is not always this dramatic but in this situation, it was very helpful to tease out the emotional from sensory regulation issues.

Now, let's take a look at Sammy.

Sammy is a 14-year-old boy who has always been a very good student. His grades are average or above, and he generally spends a lot of time studying to keep up with his work. Recently, his grades have started to slip, and he has demonstrated a lot of physical symptoms such as headaches and stomachaches. He wants to spend more and more time alone and in his room under his covers, in the dark. He has also had a lot more outbursts in which he throws things across the room, stomps his feet and slams his fist on tables. His parents and his teachers have begun to worry. He often stares into space at school and seems to be very easily distracted. He's even stopped eating certain things he's always eaten in the past, complaining that the mushy texture makes him gag.

Now that you have read the above scenario, you may want to take a moment to fill in the chart below.

Emotional Regulation Signs	Sensory Regulation Signs

Sammy is a combination of some of the older children with whom I have worked. Many of the characteristics described above are consistent with emotional concerns such as his decline in grades, desire for solitude, aggressive outbursts, physical symptoms, and inability to concentrate. It would seem appropriate for his parents to take him for further evaluation for emotional/behavioral issues.

In Sammy's case, it is apparent that there are possible emotional issues at the core of his difficulties rather than sensory. Of course, it would be important to rule this out when he was evaluated, but it seemed emotional issues might have been driving his "behavior."

I hope these examples have given you some ideas for how to sort out various developmental issues, ranging from emotional to sensory. It is important to look at a child (applies to adolescents and adults) as a whole person and make sure you are exploring each aspect of development before jumping to conclusions or putting the wrong interventions in place.

ALL
ABOUT ME

WHAT I'VE LEARNED ABOUT MYSELF

Facilitators: You and the child have made it. You have both figured out what smells, tastes, sounds, objects (visual), and textures might be bothering the child. And you've both figured out what feelings these sensory reactions may cause the child to feel.

This page and the next give you the opportunity to summarize all of this so that you and the child can refer to it when she is experiencing difficult feelings, after a challenging situation, or in anticipation of an event or interaction that may be stressful. You can help the child write the answers to the following questions. The questions are written from the perspective of the first person as I believe this will provide a more meaningful summary for your child.

My name is _____.

I have learned the following about my sensory self: _____

_____

_____

_____

_____.

I have learned that the following things cause me to feel "small" feelings: _____

_____

_____

_____

_____.

I have learned that the following things cause me to feel "medium" feelings: _____

_____

_____

_____

_____.

ALL ABOUT ME

I have learned that the following things cause me to feel "large" feelings: _____

_____

_____

_____

_____

_____.

I know the following places/situations are particularly hard for me as they seem to cause me to feel negative feelings such as uncomfortable, sad, angry, or anxious: _____

_____

_____

_____

_____

_____.

I know big, medium, and little feelings can cause my reaction to change. When I

feel intensely angry, I tend to _____. When I feel intensely
_____(over-react, under-react, react just right)_____

happy, I tend to _____. When I feel a little sad, I tend to
_____(over-react, under-react, react just right)_____

_____.
(over-react, under-react, react just right)

I have also learned that there are a lot of things I can do to help myself **feel calmer**. I will write these in my toolbox on page 126. I can also make (with or without the help of my adult) a real toolbox with these things, if I need it.

WHAT I'VE LEARNED ABOUT MYSELF

Explorers: You've made it. You have figured out what smells, tastes, sounds, objects (visual), and textures might bother you. And you have figured out what feelings these sensory reactions may cause you to feel. Better yet, you have experimented with some strategies for coping better when bombarded by sensory stimuli.

This page and the next give you the opportunity to summarize all of this so that you can refer to it when you are experiencing difficult feelings, after a challenging situation, or in anticipation of an event or interaction that may be stressful for you.

My name is _____.

I have learned the following about my sensory self: _____
_____
_____
_____
_____.

I have learned that the following things cause me to feel "small" feelings: _____
_____
_____
_____
_____.

I have learned that the following things cause me to feel "medium" feelings: _____
_____
_____
_____
_____.

ALL ABOUT ME

I have learned that the following things cause me to feel "large" feelings: _____

_____

_____

_____

_____.

I know the following places/situations are particularly hard for me as they seem to cause me to feel negative feelings such as uncomfortable, sad, angry, or anxious: _____

_____

_____

_____

_____.

I know big, medium, and little feelings can cause my reaction to change. When I

feel intensely angry, I tend to _____. When I feel intensely
(over-react, under-react, react just right)

happy, I tend to _____. When I feel a little sad, I tend to
(over-react, under-react, react just right)

_____.
(over-react, under-react, react just right)

I have also learned that there are a lot of things I can do to help myself **feel calmer**. I will write these in my toolbox on page 127. I can also make (with or without the help of my adult) a real toolbox with these things, if I need it.

MY TOOLBOX: HELPING MY BODY FEEL GREAT

✏️ **Facilitators:** In the toolbox below, help the child write or draw pictures of strategies that may help decrease his feelings and help react "just right." These items may include putty to squeeze, straws to chew, gum to chew, a candle that smells good to the child (no matches!), a stress ball to squeeze, sour-tasting candy to eat, crunchy food to eat, etc.

You can take these items and put them in a "portable toolbox" such as a plastic baggie or a pencil box. You can either obtain items that correspond to the strategies or write the strategy on a small piece of paper or index card. The child can then carry the toolbox around in his backpack so that it is easy to access. Please remind the child that it is important to use the strategy when her feelings are small or medium – before they become too big/intense to handle.

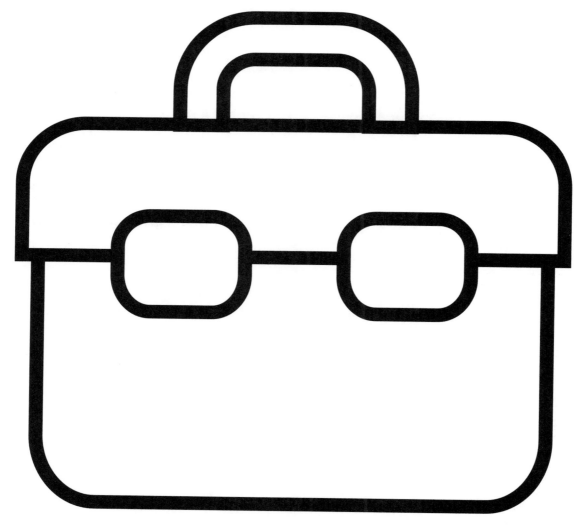

Explorers: With or without the help of an adult, you can use a container such as a pencil box, a plastic baggie, or a small backpack as your toolbox. You can then collect actual items that may help to calm your body, decrease the intensity of your feelings, and help you react "just right" and put them in your toolbox. These items may include putty to squeeze, straws to chew, gum to chew, a candle that smells good to you (no matches!), a stress ball to squeeze, sour-tasting candy to eat, crunchy food to eat, etc. You can use these items if you are having small or medium feelings to help yourself feel better before your feelings get too big/intense to handle. If it would be helpful, you can first write down the strategies you want to put into your "toolbox" on the picture below.

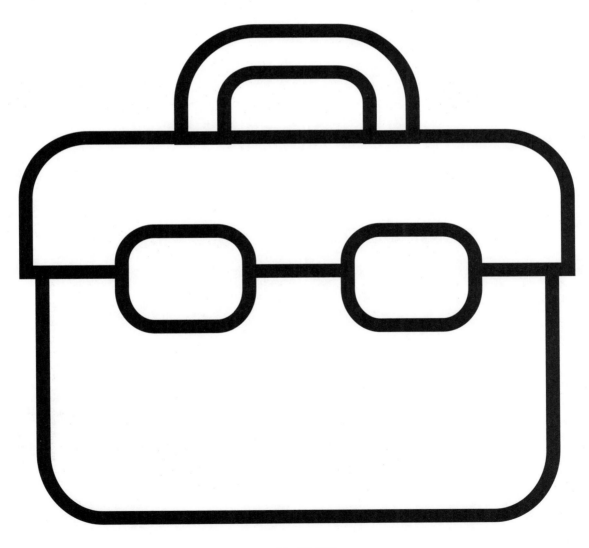

APPENDIX

Dealing with Difficult Sounds

(A "Social Story")

Facilitators: Carol Gray (1993) developed a concept called Social Stories™. Social Stories™ are a way to create understanding about a particular concept through the use of story-telling. Stories can be a very helpful way to assist children with issues they might face throughout their day as they lay out the information in a concrete, visual, memorable way. (The following story does not follow the exact format suggested by Gray.) For more information about Carol Gray, visit www.thegraycenter.org. You might want to write some stories for or with the child to help him with situations that are challenging.

Explorers: The following story may help you in situations where there are sounds that bother you. You can practice writing other stories for places or things that are hard for you. For example, if you discovered that certain smells really bother you, you can write a story to help you remember how to keep your body from over-reacting in these situations. If you are really adventurous, you can look at the following website for more information about how to write Social Stories™, developed by a woman named Carol Gray: www.thegraycenter.org. You might find this website very helpful.

Sometimes I hear sounds that bother me.

At school, I hear sounds that bother me in the cafeteria.

I hear sounds that bother me in assemblies.

I even hear sounds that bother me in the classroom.

At home, I hear sounds that bother me all of the time.

The worst sounds are the dog barking and my baby sister crying.

I start to feel really angry when I hear sounds that bother me.

My body starts to feel out of control.

At school, I know I can ask to take a break and go to the bathroom to feel better.

I know I can ask the teacher for help if I am having trouble.

At home, I know I can go to my room and put my headphones on to feel better.

I know I can go in the backyard to get away from the sounds.

I know I can ask my mom or dad for help if my body feels out of control.

I feel so much better when I do things to help my body feel better.

5-Point Scale for Voice Volume

Facilitators: Buron and Curtis's 5-Point Scale can be useful for addressing issues related to voice volume. Review the scale with the child and write in different situations in which the child participates next to the corresponding number. This may assist the child in developing a visual concept of the most appropriate voice volume associated with different situations. It may also help the child generalize this concept from situation to situation. There is a full-size chart on the next page that is easier to use.

Explorers: Have you ever noticed that people ask you to raise your voice or lower your voice even when you thought your voice was just fine? This scale might help you remember which voice volume to use in different situations. It may be helpful to think of 10 situations you commonly find yourself in, such as class, waiting rooms, the cafeteria, the library, a restaurant, etc., and write them down next to the appropriate voice volume number. This would be a good activity to do with an adult. There is a full-size chart on the next page that is easier to use.

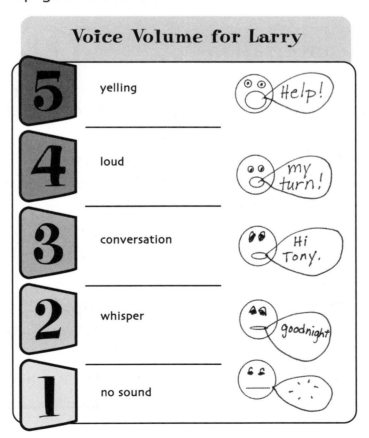

From: *The Incredible 5-Point Scale* by K. D. Buron and M. Curtis, 2004, Shawnee Mission, KS: Autism Asperger Publishing Company. Used with permission.

Voice Volume

From: *The Incredible 5-Point Scale* by K. D. Buron and M. Curtis, 2004, Shawnee Mission, KS: Autism Asperger Publishing Company. Used with permission.

GETTING TO KNOW THE CHILD'S SENSORY SELF

 For Facilitators

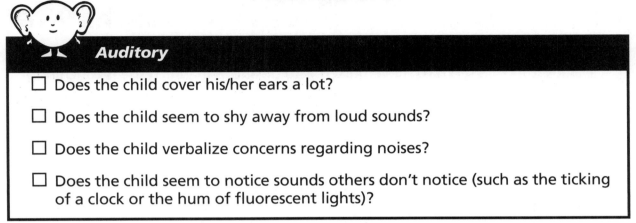

Auditory

☐ Does the child cover his/her ears a lot?

☐ Does the child seem to shy away from loud sounds?

☐ Does the child verbalize concerns regarding noises?

☐ Does the child seem to notice sounds others don't notice (such as the ticking of a clock or the hum of fluorescent lights)?

Visual

☐ Does the child hold things at odd angles to his/her eyes?

☐ Does the child move his face very close to an object when looking at it?

☐ Does the child seem to notice a light that is flickering when others don't notice it?

☐ Does the child seem to be distracted by posters and other items on the wall to the point that it interrupts his/her ability to work?

☐ Does the child seem to do better if you reduce the visual field (e.g., 10 math problems on a page versus 20)?

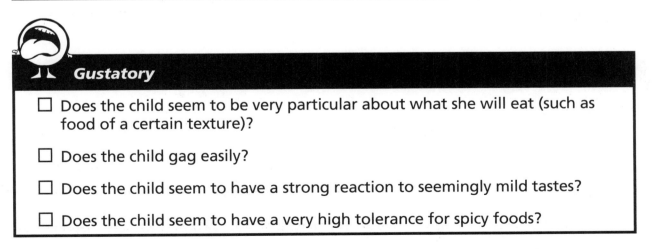

Gustatory

☐ Does the child seem to be very particular about what she will eat (such as food of a certain texture)?

☐ Does the child gag easily?

☐ Does the child seem to have a strong reaction to seemingly mild tastes?

☐ Does the child seem to have a very high tolerance for spicy foods?

Tactile

☐ Does the child seem to pull away from touch?

☐ Does the child seem to move herself into positions in which she is touching others?

☐ Does the child seem to have a particularly high threshold for pain? (e.g., falls down pretty hard but does not seem to be hurt)

☐ Does the child seem to have a particularly low threshold for pain? (e.g., gently bumps something and cries hard)

☐ Does the child seem to avoid touching certain textures?

☐ Does the child insist on washing hands immediately after touching certain textures such as paint or play dough?

Olfactory

☐ Does the child smell things repetitively?

☐ Does the child seem to notice smells that are difficult for others to perceive?

☐ Does the child seem particularly sensitive to smells to the point that she becomes distressed when she notices them?

☐ Does the child seem to have difficulty identifying and discriminating between smells?

☐ Does the child lick things that aren't appropriate to lick?

☐ Does the child gag frequently?

Vestibular

- ☐ Is the child using one hand for most tasks?
- ☐ Does the child seem like a "bull in a china shop" when moving through space?
- ☐ Can the child imitate motor movements?
- ☐ Is the child able to balance on playground equipment?
- ☐ Does the child fall down a lot?

Proprioceptive

- ☐ Is the child bumping into things or people a lot? (sensory seeking)
- ☐ Is the child able to coordinate movements such as dancing, singing songs, riding a bicycle?
- ☐ Is the child "in other people's space" a lot?
- ☐ Does the child seem to have a limited concept of others' personal space?
- ☐ Can the child imitate motor tasks? (playing such games as "Simon Says," imitating cooking in the play kitchen)

Sensory Modulation

- ☐ Does the child seem to require a lot of repetition of information?
- ☐ Does the child seem unfocused?
- ☐ Does the child take excessive risks?
- ☐ Is the child "on the go" a lot of the time?
- ☐ Does the child cover his ears?
- ☐ Does the child get agitated in crowds?

Sensory Defensiveness (Hypersensitivity)

☐ Does the child typically pull away from touch?

☐ Does the child get agitated in crowds?

☐ Does the child misperceive touch?

☐ Does the child react strongly to seemingly mild smells?

Under-Responsiveness (Hyposensitivity)

☐ Does the child seem to seek out input such as bumping into things intentionally?

☐ Does the child seem to seek input by touching things a lot?

☐ Does the child seem "out of it" or in his own world?

☐ Does the child seem tired a lot?

GETTING TO KNOW MY SENSORY SELF

 For Explorers Only

Auditory

☐ Do I cover my ears a lot?

☐ Do I tend to avoid loud sounds?

☐ Do I find myself talking a lot about noises?

☐ Do I seem to notice sounds others don't notice (such as the ticking of a clock or the hum of fluorescent lights)?

Visual

☐ Do people comment that I am holding things near my eyes in a funny way?

☐ Do people comment that I hold objects very close to my face?

☐ Do I notice lights that are flickering when others don't seem to notice them?

☐ Do I find myself distracted by posters and other items on the wall to the point that I have trouble working?

☐ Do I do better if someone gives me less to focus on on a page?

Gustatory

☐ Is it hard for me to eat certain textures?

☐ Do I gag easily?

☐ Do some tastes really bother me more than other people who are eating the same thing?

☐ Do people comment on how I can eat things that are really spicy?

Tactile

☐ Is it hard for me to tolerate other people touching me?

☐ Do people ask me to move out of their space because I am touching them?

☐ Do I have a really high threshold for pain? (It takes a lot for me to feel pain)

☐ Do I have a really low threshold for pain? (I feel pain very quickly)

☐ Do I find myself avoiding certain textures such as sand, grass, paint, slimy foods?

☐ Do I feel like I have to wash my hands immediately after touching something like sand, paint, or slimy food?

Olfactory

☐ Do people comment on my holding things up to my nose to smell them a lot?

☐ Do I notice smells that others do not seem to notice?

☐ Do a lot of smells really bother me?

☐ Is it hard for me to determine what I am smelling?

☐ Have I gotten in trouble (or tried to avoid getting in trouble) for licking something I wasn't supposed to lick?

☐ Do I gag a lot?

Vestibular

☐ Do I use one hand for most tasks?

☐ Do I bump into a lot of things by accident? (Do people sometimes say I'm like a bull in a china shop?)

☐ Can I imitate motor movements such as if someone tries to teach me a new dance or a new move in sports?

☐ Can I, or was I able to balance on playground equipment?

☐ Do I trip or fall down a lot?

Proprioceptive

☐ Does it feel good when I bump into people or things?

☐ Was it, or is it still hard for me to dance, ride a bicycle?

☐ Do people tell me I am in their "space" a lot?

☐ Is it hard for me to understand what "personal space" really means?

☐ Was it, or is it hard for me to play "Simon Says," or imitate what other people are doing with their bodies?

Sensory Modulation

☐ Do I need information repeated to me a lot?

☐ Is it hard for me to focus?

☐ Do I take a lot of risks?

☐ Am I always "on the go"?

☐ Do I cover my ears a lot?

☐ Do crowds make me feel uncomfortable?

Sensory Defensiveness (Hypersensitivity)

☐ Does touch bother me to the point that I tend to pull away from it?

☐ Do a lot of people in one space bother me?

☐ Does touch often feel uncomfortable to me? (such as a teacher putting a hand on my shoulder)

☐ Do smells bother me a lot?

Under-Responsiveness (Hyposensitivity)

☐ Do I like to bump into things intentionally (seek input)?

☐ Do I like to touch things a lot?

☐ Do I sometimes feel out of it and in my own world?

☐ Do I feel tired a lot?

FEELINGS CHART

Positive Feelings		
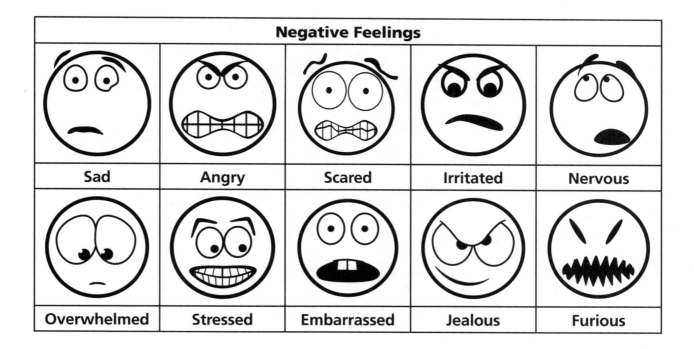		
Happy	Excited	Surprised
Thrilled	Calm	Relaxed

Negative Feelings				
Sad	Angry	Scared	Irritated	Nervous
Overwhelmed	Stressed	Embarrassed	Jealous	Furious

Feelings Thermometer

0 1 2 3 4 5

Sample Picture of My Sensory Body

Overly sensitive to loud noises ...

Bumps into people in line ...

Has difficulty paying attention ...

Has difficulty with hair washing and brushing ...

Picky eater ...

Always "on the go" ...

Problems with handwriting ...

Only likes certain types of clothing ...

Clumsy ...

From: *Asperger Syndrome and Sensory Issues – Practical Solutions for Making Sense of the World* by B. S. Myles, K. T. Cook, N. E. Miller, L. Rinner, and L. A. Robbins, 2000, Shawnee Mission, KS: Autism Asperger Publishing Company. Used with permission.

Pictures of My Body

Over-React

Pictures of My Body

Under-React

Pictures of My Body

"Just Right"

Sample Sensory Stimuli

cars/trucks/jeeps/traffic

rain

buzzing/bright lights

plants/inside/outside

water/getting wet

ceiling fans/other fans

motorcycles

music

standing in line/
others too close

fire alarm/other alarms

fruit/veggies/
foods I don't like

mushy/things I don't
like touching

crowds

bad smells

seeing my favorite toy

Facilitator: You may want to laminate the pictures and cut them out for ease of use in various situations.

MY CUP RUNNETH OVER

The "Piggyback" Effect of Triggers, Stimuli, and Feelings

Facilitators and **Explorers:** It can be helpful to view our bodies as having a "cup" inside of them in which feelings, stimuli, and triggers can build to the point of overflowing. If we *empty* the cup regularly, we can keep our bodies reacting "just right." If our cup gets too full, we may over-react or under-react. This might cause our bodies to move too fast or too slow. We can *empty* our cups by choosing strategies that help decrease the level of feelings in our cups.

To do this activity, you will need a cup, a pitcher of water, and a bowl. Place the cup in the bowl and put the pitcher next to it.

Facilitators: Introduce this activity to the child by saying: "We are going to pretend that this cup is in my body and that it holds all of my stress and big feelings. The water is the triggers and big feelings. When I got out of bed this morning, I stubbed my toe really hard. (pour a bit of water in the cup) When I went to get breakfast, the cereal box was empty. UGH, that's my favorite cereal! (pour a bit of water in the cup) I kept myself calm, though, and walked over to get some juice, but the juice container was empty. (pour lots of water in the cup) I sat down and tried to stay calm, but just then my daughter started yelling for me." (overflow the cup)

It is most effective if you let the water spill for a moment before you stop pouring. (The bowl will catch the excess water.) Discuss each trigger and talk about what strategies may have helped prevent the cup from overflowing. Have the child take a turn and talk about triggers in a similar way while you or the child fills the cup.

Explorers: This is a good activity to do with an adult so you can talk through it together. Think about things that triggered you to feel negative feelings such as anger, frustration, sadness, and worries. For each trigger you think of, pour water into the cup. Once the cup begins to overflow, stop pouring water.

Now think about strategies that might have helped you feel better in each of the situations you thought of. Do you think those strategies could have kept your cup from overflowing?

Sensory Integration – A Brief Historical Overview

Clinician	Title of Work/Date of Work	Summary
A. Jean Ayres, Ph.D., OTR	*Sensory Integration and the Child* (1979)	Dr. Ayres posited that behavior issues sometimes resulted from the central nervous system's inability to accurately interpret sensory input, thus causing inappropriate responses to the input. She not only examined this as it relates to the five senses but also examined the proprioceptive and vestibular systems (see Chapter 3 for more information) and the ways in which our bodies know how to accomplish more complex motor skills such as kicking a ball, jumping, and buttoning a button. Dr. Ayres' work created a map from which many occupational therapists have built and refined interventions to help struggling children. Dr. Ayres has written many other books and articles. For more information, please see http://www.siglobalnetwork.org/about.htm or http://www.spdfoundation.net.
Winnie Dunn, Ph.D., OTR, FAOTA	*Sensory Profile for Infants and Toddlers* (2002) *Adolescent/Adult Sensory Profile* (2002) (with Catana E. Brown) *Sensory Profile School Companion* (2006)	These tools assist clinicians in assessing sensory patterns and responses to life events.
Patricia Wilbarger, MEd, OTR, FAOTA	The Wilbarger Brushing Protocol *Sensory defensiveness in children aged 2-12.* (1991) (With Julia Wilbarger)	Patricia Wilbarger, MEd, OTR, FAOTA, has examined and developed strategies for sensory defensiveness. Dr. Wilbarger developed a protocol for assisting children in decreasing their defensive response, called The Wilbarger Brushing Protocol. For more information about Dr. Wilbarger's work, please see the following website: http://www.childdevelopmentmedia.com/avanti_educational_programs.html.

Sensory Integration – A Brief Historical Overview (continued)

Clinician	Title of Work/Date of Work	Summary
Mary Sue Williams, OTR/L, and Sherry Shellenberger, OTR/L	*How Does Your Engine Run?® A Leader's Guid to The Alert Program® for Self-Regulation* (1996)	In 1996, Mary Sue Williams, OTR/L, and Sherry Shellenberger, OTR/L published *How Does Your Engine Run?® A Leader's Guide to The Alert Program® for Self-Regulation* in which they compared the human body to an engine to describe the complicated process of self-regulation. This program, called the *Alert Program®*, offers parents, teachers, and clinicians a framework from which to assist children with self-regulation.
Carol Stock Kranowitz, MA	*The Out-of-Sync Child: Recognizing and Coping with Sensory Integration Dysfunction* (1998)	*The Out-of-Sync Child* was published following Kranowitz' work with Dr. Lynn Balzer-Martin (who trained with Dr. Ayres) to assist families with working on goals in the sensory arena at their own pace through concrete activities that address different areas of sensory processing and development. The activities can be easily be used in many different setting such as schools, home and the general community. Dr. Kranowitz has also published a variety of other books in this area.
Interdisciplinary Council on Developmental and Learning Disabilities (ICDL) Stanley Greenspan, MD, Serena Wieder, Ph.D.	*Diagnostic Classification: Zero to Three: Diagnostic Classification of Mental Health in Developmental Disorders in Infancy and Early Childhood* (2006) *Diagnostic Manual for Infancy and Early Childhood* (2007)	Dr. Lucy Jane Miller spearheaded the inclusion of sensory processing disorder (SPD) in both of these diagnostic manuals.
Lucy Jane Miller, Ph.D., OTR	*Miller Assessment for Preschoolers (MAP)* (1982) *Sensational Kids: Hope and Help for Children with Sensory Processing Disorders* (2006)	Dr. Miller, Ph.D., OTR. and a group of other clinicians, including but not limited to: Margaret Bauman, MD, and Edward J. Goldson, MD, are members of the Sensory Processing Disorder (SPD) Scientific Work Group and are engaged in research around many different aspects of SPD. Dr. Miller is leading a movement advocating inclusion of sensory processing disorder in the *Diagnostic Statistical Manual-V (DSM-V)* in 2012. For more information, see http://www.spdfoundation.net.

References and Resources

The following books are in no way an exhaustive list of books that cover sensory issues, feelings, and strategies. I am including these titles because I have found them helpful in my practice with children and their families. The books are clear, straightforward, insightful, and easy to adapt for use with many different life situations, diagnostic issues, and settings.

Attwood, T. (2004). *Exploring feelings: Cognitive behaviour therapy to manage anger.* Arlington, TX: Future Horizons.

Attwood, T. (2004). *Exploring feelings: Cognitive behaviour therapy to manage anxiety.* Arlington, TX: Future Horizons.

With these two books, Attwood provides a program through which children and adolescents may explore their feelings. Based on cognitive behavioral principles, the program is designed to help children manage anxiety and anger, but it would be helpful for other emotions as well. Easy-to-use worksheets can be used by children and adolescents independently or with the help of an adult.

Ayres, A. J. (2005). *Sensory integration and the child.* Los Angeles: Western Psychological Services.

In this reprint of Ayres' earlier work, she describes sensory integration both in terms of function and dysfunction. She discusses examples of sensory issues in a variety of areas and links sensory integration dysfunction to different areas of need a child may experience.

Buron, K. D. (2007). *A "5" could make me lose control!* Shawnee Mission, KS: Autism Asperger Publishing Company.

In this simple yet powerful workbook, Buron has created a way to more closely examine situations that may occur in a child's life and the level or intensity of stress these situations may cause. The book consists of an interactive 1 to 5 stress scale that contains pockets in which the child can place descriptions of stressful situations. This enables the child to visually see the level of stress or anxiety these situations may cause. Guidance is provided around assisting children with finding strategies that will help them manage their stress and anxiety.

Buron, K. D., & Curtis, M. (2004). *The incredible 5-point scale: Assisting students with autism spectrum disorders in understanding social interactions and controlling their emotional responses.* Shawnee Mission, KS: Autism Asperger Publishing Company.

Buron and Curtis offer a straightforward, easy-to-use system for assisting children in dealing with their emotions. The book gives children and the adults who work with them a way to better define goals, understand the behavior that interferes with the goals, and actually meet the goals.

Cardon, T. (2004). *Let's talk emotions. Helping children with social cognitive deficits, including AS, HFA, and NVLD, learn to understand and express empathy and emotions.* Shawnee Mission, KS: Autism Asperger Publishing Company.

Designed for children ages 4 to 18, the activities in Cardon's book teach children to identify and respond to their own feelings as well as the feelings of others. In the process, they improve their chances of establishing and maintaining fulfilling and successful social relationships.

Gabriels, R., & Hill, D. (2002). *Autism: From research to individualized practice.* London: Jessica Kingsley Publishers.

In this book a variety of clinicians speak to the many areas of need of children with autism spectrum disorders. Each chapter includes wonderful ideas for working with children around such issues as occupational therapy needs, sibling issues, and speech/language concerns.

Gabriels, R., & Hill, D. (2007). *Growing up with autism: Working with school-age children and adolescents.* New York: The Guilford Press.

This is an indispensable resource for working with older children and adolescents. The contributors to the book cover subjects including, but not limited to, behavior, communication, social skills, sexuality, and educational needs.

Gray, C. (1993). *The original social story™ book.* Arlington, TX: Future Horizons.

Carol Gray has created a unique way to impart information to children and adolescents to help them learn social rules, daily routines, and other information that will assist them with their everyday lives. Social Stories™ can be very helpful with sensory issues and emotional difficulties.

Greenspan, S. I. (2005). *Diagnostic manual for infancy and early childhood.* Bethesda, MD: Interdisciplinary Council on Developmental and Learning Disabilities.

The Interdisciplinary Council on Developmental and Learning Disabilities founded by Stanley Greenspan, MD, and Serena Wieder, Ph.D., published this diagnostic manual to describe neurodevelopmental (including autism spectrum disorders), mental health, regulatory-sensory processing, language disorders and learning challenges in young children.

Greenspan, S.I., & Wieder, S. (Eds.). (2005). *Diagnostic manual for infancy and early childhood: Mental health, developmental, regulatory-sensory processing, language and learning disorders – ICDL-DMIC.* Bethesda, MD: Interdisciplinary Council on Developmental and Learning Disorders (ICDL).

This and ZERO TO THREE were the first diagnostic manuals to explore diagnoses in the birth-to-three population.

Gutstein, S. E. (2001). *Autism Asperger Syndrome: Solving the relationship puzzle – A new developmental program that opens the door to lifelong social and emotional growth.* Arlington, TX: Future Horizons.

With this book, Dr. Gutstein introduces a new way of viewing the development of relationship skills in people on the autism spectrum. He talks about the importance of assisting people with autism to experience the rush of hormones associated with a positive interaction so that they become "addicted" to interactions. His book offers helpful developmental milestones as well as games to assist with the development of relationship skills.

Hall, K. (2001). *Asperger syndrome, the universe and everything.* London: Jessica Kingsley Publishers.

Kenneth Hall wrote this book when he was 10 years old to describe his experience as a child with Asperger Syndrome. The book gives the reader the opportunity to step into Kenneth's world and see it from his perspective. He includes some very encouraging descriptions of his interactions with the sensory world around him.

Jaffe, A., & Gardner, L. (2006). *My book full of feelings. How to control and react to the size of your emotions.* Shawnee Mission, KS: Autism Asperger Publishing Company.

This book is fully interactive and uses a dry-erase marker so that unique situations can be added and changed with a wipe of a paper towel as the child masters a skill and grows. The book also includes communication sheets for tracking and sharing information between home and school.

Jackson, L. (2002). *Freaks, geeks and Asperger Syndrome: A user guide to adolescence.* London: Jessica Kingsley Publishers.

Luke Jackson writes about life as a 13-year-old with Asperger Syndrome. He relates to adolescents in a way that adults could not as he shares his wisdom and insight about his experiences. He offers some very helpful descriptions about sensory systems and the impact his sensory struggles have on him.

Korin, E.S.H. (2006). *Asperger Syndrome – An owner's manual: What you, your parents and your teachers need to know.* Shawnee Mission, KS: Autism Asperger Publishing Company.

Asperger Syndrome – An Owner's Manual provides fifth to eighth graders an opportunity to work with an adult to explore and get to know themselves. This interactive workbook takes children on a journey through thought-provoking worksheets, questions, and concrete concepts so that they can formulate their own personal profile as a child with Asperger Syndrome.

Korin, E.S.H. (2007). *Asperger Syndrome: An owner's manual 2 – For older adolescents and adults: What you, your parents and friends, and your employer, need to know.* Shawnee Mission, KS: Autism Asperger Publishing Company.

In this second edition, Korin expands the interactive worksheets, helpful information and tips from her earlier book. The workbook helps older adolescents and adults become more familiar with themselves—their strengths, challenges, and goals—as a stepping stone for developing strategies to achieve their goals.

Kranowitz, C. S. (1998). *The out-of-sync child: Recognizing and coping with sensory integration dysfunction.* New York: Skylight Press.

This comprehensive resource examines the concept of sensory integration dysfunction. Kranowitz's straightforward style along with examples and descriptions give a helpful overview of the different components of the sensory system as well as a clear picture of sensory dysfunction. The book includes information that pertains to the multitude of environments children enter and offers encouraging statements from parents with children with sensory integration dysfunction.

153

Kranowitz, C. S. (2003*). The out-of-sync child has fun: Activities for kids with sensory process-ing disorder. New York: Penguin Group Inc.

With this book, Kranowitz has taken her first book (*The Out-of-Sync Child*) a giant step further, offering activities that assist children with difficulties in the various areas of sensory processing. The user-friendly activities appeal to children despite their sensory difficulties. Given the ease with which most of the activities can be set up, they are useful both in school and home environ-ments.

McAfee, J. (2002). *Navigating the social world: A curriculum for individuals with Asperger's Syndrome, high functioning autism and related disorders.* Arlington, TX: Future Horizons.

McAfee offers a multitude of helpful strategies for working with children on the autism spectrum or with similar characteristics. The book is user friendly and provides visual ways to approach many areas of concern, including, but not limited to, recognizing and understanding emotions, social skills, behavior, stress, and communication.

Miller, L. J., Cermak, S., Lane, S., Alzalone, M., & Koomer, J. (2004, Summer). Position statement on terminology related to sensory integration dysfunction. *S.I. Focus*, 6-8.

Miller et al. propose a new diagnostic terminology that distinguishes the terms used for diagnoses from the terms use to describe treatment and theory. They propose the term *sensory processing disorder* as the umbrella for three different categories of diagnoses under which there are five different subgroups.

Miller, Lucy Jane, & Fuller, Doris A. (2006). *Sensational kids: Hope and help for children with sensory processing disorder (SPD).* New York: The Penguin Group.

This reader-friendly book identifies sensory processing disorder (SPD) and its four major subtypes, along with information about assessment and diagnosis, treatment options, and strategies, in-cluding the importance of occupational therapy and parental involvement. The authors offer hope and advice to parents on how to be the best possible advocates for their children.

Myles, B. S., Cook, K. T., Miller, N. E., Rinner, L., & Robbins, L. A. (2000). *Asperger Syndrome and sensory issues: Practical solutions for making sense of the world.* Shawnee Mission, KS: Autism Asperger Publishing Company.

Myles et al. have created a wonderful visual way to think about sensory issues with the "sensory gang." These helpful characters follow you through the book as the authors shed light on the specifics of the different nuances of our sensory systems. The book also breaks down specific be-haviors and possible explanations for these behaviors, and presents strategies that may decrease the behaviors. The book offers assistance with helping children both in school, in public, and at home.

Sher, B. (2006). *Attention games.* San Francisco: Jossey-Bass.

This book outlines activities that may be useful in increasing a child's ability to concentrate and attend. The activities are divided by age and are relatively simple to replicate. Some of the activi-ties are helpful for a child experiencing sensory issues.

Stackhouse, T. M., Graham, N. S., & Laschober, J. S. (2002). Occupational therapy intervention and autism. In R. L. Gabriels & D. E. Hill (Eds.), *Autism – From research to individualised practice* (pp. 155-177). London: Jessica Kingsley Publishers, Ltd.

This chapter offers helpful information about sensory integration dysfunction. Although written to highlight the role of occupational therapy in the treatment of a child with an autism spectrum disorder, it is broader in scope, to include key concepts in sensory integration in general. It also offers some very helpful case examples.

Stallard, P. (2002). *Think good-feel good: A cognitive behaviour therapy workbook for children and young people.* West Sussex, England: John Wiley & Sons, Inc.

Stallard has created a device that can be used to assist children in exploring their feelings, behaviors, and ability to problem solve. The worksheets, strategies, and tools are based on the principles of cognitive behavioral therapy and are laid out in a clear, visual way.

Wilbarger, P., & Wilbarger, J. L. (1991). *Sensory defensiveness in children aged 2-12*. Santa Barbara, CA: Avanti Educational Programs.

This brief text provides information regarding sensory defensiveness, including the definition, levels of severity, intervention approaches, and other helpful information specifically related to sensory defensiveness.

Williams, M. S., & Shellenberger, S. (1996). *"How does your engine run?"® A leader's guide to the Alert Program® for self-regulation*. Albuquerque, NM: TherapyWorks.

Williams and Shellenberger describe how to move from difficulties with body control to self-regulation. The book compares a person's body to an engine, which provides a helpful illustration of the complex process of self-regulation.

Zero to Three. (1994). *Diagnostic classification of mental health in developmental disorders in infancy and early childhood.* Arlington, VA: Author.

ZERO TO THREE Diagnostic Classification Task Force, Greenspan, S. I. (chair), Wieder, S. (co-chair and clinical director). (1994). *Diagnostic classification of mental health and developmental disorders of infancy and early childhood.* Arlington, VA: ZERO TO THREE/National Center for Clinical Infant Programs.

Samples of Children's Books for Exploring Feelings

The following books either explore feelings specifically or include feelings as part of the storyline.

Alborough, Jez. (2000). *Hug.* Cambridge, MA: Candlewick Press.

This book is a wonderful, nearly nonverbal story about a monkey's feelings as he journeys toward receiving a hug of his own.

Bang, Molly. (1999). *When Sophie gets angry – really, really angry . . .* New York: Scholastic Inc.

Bang takes her readers through the trigger that caused Molly to feel angry, the strategy she chooses, and what happens as she begins to feel better.

Berry, Joy. (1995). *Let's talk about feeling afraid.* New York: Scholastic Inc.

Berry offers some clear examples of things that might cause someone to feel afraid.

Buron, K. D. (2005). *When my worries get too big! A relaxation book for children who live with anxiety.* Shawnee Mission, KS: Autism Asperger Publishing Company.

This is a wonderful tool that can be used to help children recognize the intensity of their worries and determine strategies that might be helpful. The pictures are quite descriptive, and the opportunity to personalize the book is very beneficial to a child.

Cain, Janan. (2000). *The way I feel.* New York: Scholastic Inc.

Cain describes a range of feelings that are accompanied by wonderful pictures.

Carle, Eric. (1995). *The very lonely firefly.* New York: Philomel.

Carle tells a tale of the adventures of a firefly as he tries to find others who are like him.

Cronin, Doreen, & Lewin, Betsy. (2002). *Giggle, giggle quack.* New York: Simon & Schuster.

In this funny book, Cronin tells of a very smart duck who changes things around while the farmer is away. It illustrates happiness, excitement, frustration, and anger.

Curtis, Jamie Lee. (1998). *Today I feel silly: and other moods that make my day.* New York: Harper Collins.

Curtis describes many different emotions to the accompaniment of wonderful drawings by Laura Cornell.

Drachman, Eric. (2005). *A frog thing.* Los Angeles: Kidwick Books LLS.

In this unique book Drachman describes a frog's feelings over wanting to do something that others tell him he is incapable of doing.

James, Brian. (2002). *The shark who was afraid of everything.* New York: Scholastic Inc.

James offers a range of emotions in this sweet tale of a shark who learns to find his courage.

Larson, Elaine. (2008). *The chameleon kid.* Shawnee Mission, KS: Autism Asperger Publishing Company.

In whimsical verse accompanied by strong illustrations, the Chameleon Kid in the story by the same name shows how to control Meltdown, the monster who is always lying in wait, before Meltdown takes control.

Lears, Laurie. (1998). *Ian's walk: A story about autism.* Morton Grove, IL: Albert Whitman and Company.

In this poignant book, Lears takes her reader on a walk with Ian and his sisters. On the walk, we take a tour of Ian's sensory system and become more aware of the things he is noticing through his five senses. We also get to share his siblings' feelings of anger, love, fear, and frustration as they walk with Ian.

LeSieg, Theo. (1961). *Ten apples up on top!* New York: Random House.

In this cute story, LeSieg (a.k.a. Theodor Geisel a.k.a. Dr. Seuss) writes about animals competing with each other to have more apples "up on top" of their heads. It is packed with wonderful cartoon-like feelings and feeling faces.

Lithgow, John. (2000). *The remarkable Farkle McBride.* New York: Simon & Schuster.

This wonderful story tells of a little boy exploring his musical talent, the frustrations he encounters, and the moment when he finally feels content.

Mayer, Gina, & Mayer, Mercer. (1995). *Just a bad day.* New York: Golden Books Publishing Company, Inc.

Just a Bad Day describes the different emotions Little Critter has as he goes through a very hard day filled with disappointments and challenges.

Mayer, Mercer. (2006). *Just so thankful.* New York: HarperFestival.

In this touching book, Mayer includes many emotions (as most of his books do) as he tells the tale of Little Critter learning about what is really important.

Murrell, Diane. (2006). *Oliver Onion: The onion who learns to accept and be himself.* Shawnee Mission, KS: Autism Asperger Publishing Company.

In this illustrated children's book, Oliver Onion faces situations familiar to all children, including children on the autism spectrum. In particular, it illustrates feeling scared in a helpful, educational way.

Penn, Audrey. (1993). *The kissing hand.* Washington, DC: Child & Family Press.

This is a wonderful story of the difficulties children encounter when trying to separate from their parents. Penn not only highlights the trigger of the emotions as well as the actual emotions, but also offers a very helpful strategy for separation issues.

Snodgrass, Catherine. (2008). *What's that look? All about faces and feelings.* Shawnee Mission, KS: Autism Asperger Publishing Company.

This richly illustrated book connects faces to feelings while building a larger vocabulary of words to identify feelings. With one "look" per page, each page presents a scene in which the emotion is appropriately explained.

Spelman, Cornelia Maude. (2000). *When I feel angry.* New York: Scholastic, Inc.

Spelman talks about anger in a very helpful way.

Veenendall, Jennifer. (2008). *Arnie and his school tools: Simple sensory solutions that build success.* Shawnee Mission, KS: Autism Asperger Publishing Company.

This illustrated children's book shows Arnie finding tools that help him deal with his sensory challenges at school and at home in a natural, straightforward way.

Viorst, Judith. (1972). *Alexander and the terrible, horrible, no good, very bad day.* New York: Scholastic Inc.

This well-known book includes wonderful feeling faces and descriptions of a variety of feelings.

Viorst, Judith. (1987). *Alexander, who used to be rich last Sunday.* New York: Aladdin Paperbacks.

In this book, Viorst again offers a story chock full of triggers and feelings.

Willems, Mo. (2004). *Knuffle bunny.* New York: Scholastic, Inc.

This adorable book tells the tale of a little girl who has lost her bunny in the laundromat. It includes a whole host of clearly depicted feelings.

Wilson, Karma. (2002). *Bear snores on.* New York: Margaret K. McElderry.

In this sweet book, Wilson tells the story of a bear who sleeps through a party in his "very own lair." It illustrates anger, fear, joy and happiness through its wonderfully rhythmic rhymes.

Wood, Audrey. (1985). *King Bidgood's in the bathtub.* New York: Harcourt, Inc.

This story of a king who will not get out of the tub includes some wonderful feelings and feeling faces.

Wood, Audrey, & Wood, Bruce. (1984). *The little mouse, the red ripe strawberry, and the big hungry bear.* New York: Scholastic, Inc.

This is a story of a mouse who finds a strawberry and is quite excited until he finds out about the bear who wants to eat it. The book is chock full of wonderful feeling faces.

Wood, Audrey, & Wood, Bruce. (2003). *Alphabet mystery.* New York: The Blue Sky Press.

Most of Audrey and Bruce Wood's books include descriptions of triggers and feelings. In *Alphabet Mystery,* the Woods describe the letters attempting to solve the mystery of the missing I's dot.

Yolen, Jane, & Teague, Mark. (2000). *How do dinosaurs say good night?* New York: Scholastic, Inc.

Jane Yolen and Mark Teague have written a series of dinosaur books that illustrate feelings around typical situations such as saying good night, making friends, and going to school.

APC

Autism Asperger Publishing Co.
P.O. Box 23173
Shawnee Mission, Kansas 66283-0173
www.asperger.net • 913-897-1004